Powering India to Double Digit Growth: Five Key Steps to a Robust Economy

Ramesh S Arunachalam

First published in The United States of America on January 1, 2020 by Shruthikka Media World

Copyright © 2020 Ramesh S Arunachalam.

Ramesh S Arunachalam has the complete moral right to be identified as author of this work, which presents his original ideas, analysis and writings. Contact: shruthika438@gmail.com

Cover Design: K Ravindran
Research Assistance: SP Pandiyan

Copyright Information

Ramesh S Arunachalam claims copyright only with the original writings, ideas, interpretation, and analysis done by the author, Ramesh S Arunachalam. No copyright is claimed with regard to any material that is cited or quoted—which are very, very negligible anyways (see appendix 4). In fact, 99.99 percent of the book comprises of original thoughts, ideas and analysis.

Dedication

This book is dedicated to my late mother, *Jaya Arunachalam*, who was everything to me and who taught me everything in life including compassion and empathy for fellow human beings the world over. The book is also dedicated to my close friend, Mr V. Ananth, who was instrumental in my writing this book.

Contents

	Introduction	1
Chapter 1	Abolish Income Tax, Introduce a Banking Transactions' Tax (BTT) and Rationalize the Goods and Services Tax (GST)	8
Chapter 2	Reduce Stamp Duty on Property and Revise Property Guideline Values	41
Chapter 3	Restructure the Lokpal and Lokayuktas	67
Chapter 4	Create a Sound and Effective Public Procurement Act	89
Chapter 5	Reform the Political Economy	101
Chapter 6	Conclusion	125
	Appendices	171

Foreword

"If winter comes, can spring be far behind?" is the prophetic hope voiced by P. B. Shelley. What holds good for Nature can be true of the market too, provided remedial measures are taken in right earnest.

The economy worldwide is facing a downturn. India is also taking a big hit. What is to be done now? Subramanian Swamy has come out with his "RESET" so that the nation can regain its economic legacy. Nobel laureates Abhijit V Banerjee and Esther Duflo have laid down their prescriptions in *Good Economics for Hard Times*. Ramesh Arunachalam joins them with his tract for the times.

Ramesh has to be read for more reasons than one. The book is strikingly original with a pragmatic flavor. It is comprehensive in its sweep. Ramesh adopts an integral approach. To go back to Shelley, "Nothing in the world is single;/All things by a law divine/In one spirit meet and mingle". The parts of the human body from head to toe are organically linked.

The economy is no different. Ramesh recognizes this integral element of the economy. He notes, for instance, that the real estate sector which is critical for achieving growth and which impacts more than 250 manufacturing and service industries, including steel and cement can be vibrant and growing only if guideline values, stamp duties, registration charges and taxes are rationalized. This segment is also a big generator of black money. Corruption and black money are intertwined. Therefore, the Lokpal and Lokayuktas have to be restructured by providing them with more teeth. A holistic reform of the political economy is necessary to power India to achieve greater growth.

There is an eternal debate between growth and market on the one hand and welfare and distribution on the other. In fact, there is no fundamental conflict between these two sets of values. We have been laying too much emphasis on welfare and distribution. But, unless there is a fresh generation of resources and achievement of greater growth, there will be very little left in the end for distribution and meeting the goals of welfare. Hence, it is essential to listen to the author's counsel, which will propel India into a high growth trajectory, through innovative mechanisms including the rationalization of Income Tax and the Goods and Services Tax.

Ramesh has been meditating, reflecting and articulating on economic issues for the last several years. He has had a very wide exposure. He has worked extensively on the ground, both within and outside India. He was the earliest to warn about the predatory approach of some micro-finance institutions. He even wrote a novel with that theme. He has a sound theoretical grasp. He has been churning out book after book.

This latest one is his best. Ramesh does not believe in breast-beating. He is always sanguine about the future. This book is more a manifesto for economic prosperity. Its theme is that unless we achieve double digit growth, we cannot eradicate poverty. I am sure that this book will be widely read and also receive the personal and serious attention of the policy makers.

I congratulate Ramesh Arunachalam on his wonderful work.

Justice G. R. Swaminathan
Judge, Madras High Court

x

Introduction

In the last 72 years, much has been attempted in India to push the country towards economic growth and prosperity while at the same time trying to reduce poverty and associated inequality. While we have had some successes, India largely remains a dualistic economy with huge inequality and real wealth is concentrated in the hands of a few. For this and other reasons, India has never been able to have annual GDP[1] growth rates consistently in double

---

[1] GDP, Gross Domestic Product, is a monetary measure of the market value of all final goods and services produced in a period (quarterly or yearly).

digits, required to eliminate poverty,[2] and more importantly vulnerability.[3]

Part of the reason for the above is the fact that India has always embraced some form of populist economics, which has well-known drawbacks. It is here that India must observe and learn from a staunch socialist country like China, that has adapted itself and become a true, yet sensitive and market-friendly economy with reasonable, if not spectacular success. There is much to be learned from the above experience and it is time India does that and abandons its traditional model of economic populism, steeped in its tradition since independence.

India needs to adapt and create its own brand of economic governance, suited uniquely to its socio-cultural traditions. Only this will help unleash the grassroots driven entrepreneurial spirit required to power India to double digit growth that can not only eliminate poverty but also reduce inequality and thereby contribute immensely to the United Nation's

---

[2] In my opinion, to eliminate poverty completely, India's GDP will have to grow at annual rates exceeding 15 percent and it is surely possible as the recommendations in this book suggest.

[3] Vulnerability is a unique and critical construct. People, who have moved beyond the poverty line, may however become poor with one life cycle event—be it a setback, emergency or any other issue for that matter. For example, a perfectly well-to-do family could be burdened by a huge debt and lose all assets if their breadwinner suffers a serious health setback or were to die. Thus, in my experience, across the 640 districts of India and 31 countries globally over the last thirty years, I have witnessed life cycle events impacting well-to-do families, causing them severe economic despair.

Sustainable Development Goals[4] (UNSDG) # 1 and # 10.

While the above describes the general issues in the context of India's economic growth, the present condition of the economy is especially precarious and extremely worrying.[5] Consumer spending is at an all-time low and exports are declining. Manufacturing output is also on shaky ground and the markets have been in a state of deep fluctuation—alternating between upward and downward spirals. While one can go on and elaborate the causes for the above, it is difficult because the real reasons are multiple and span several decades. **Anyway, much post mortem has occurred and that is not the purpose here**. Rather, this effort takes a constructive approach and outlines practical steps and reforms by which India can consistently have an annual GDP growth rate in the double digits exceeding 15 percent in real terms in the years to come.

In doing the above, this effort also suggests practical and implementable strategies using my grassroots, multi-level and multi-sectoral experience from 640 districts of India and 31 other countries spread over 30 years. I also use the lessons from my vicarious learning. Sub-questions explored include (but are not limited to) the following:

a) How to rationalize the **direct and indirect tax regime and enhance revenue generation** while

---

[4] Please see appendix 3 for an explanation of the UNSDGs.
[5] Please see appendix 1b for comprehensive data on the same, which is self-explanatory.

at the same time make it less burdensome for the citizens?

b) How to bring the **parallel economy in the real estate and infrastructure sector into the formal economy** and eliminate the vast hoards of black money and corruption in real estate?

c) How to **fight and prevent regular and spectacular corruption so that the parallel (black) economy is eliminated** and the country as a whole benefits?

d) How to make the political system **more accountable, effective and efficient** so that they can seamlessly contribute to India having a vibrant democracy, which, in turn, can assist the move towards double digit GDP growth and a resilient economy?

While it is tempting to talk of all of the above issues here, I think, for the purposes of this introductory chapter, it is sufficient to mention that five key big bang steps (as outlined in the succeeding chapters and conclusion) are necessarily required to push the Indian economy into a high growth trajectory. Without a doubt, these five big bang steps must be implemented—otherwise the Indian economy will continue to remain in its current state of inertia, of slow growth and other associated symptoms, as elaborated here.

Accordingly, the remainder of this book unfolds as follows:

Chapter # 1 explores the income tax conundrum and suggests practical ways in which India's tax system can be rationalized to eliminate black money generation. The need is to move from the existing complex income tax system to one that is simple, cost effective and transparent with lower transaction costs and greater ease of operation for both the government and the taxpayer. The chapter also examines practical ways in which the existing/accumulated black money reserves—whether in India or abroad and/or stored in other forms like real estate, jewels, stocks, shares etc.,–can be mopped up without a loss to the exchequer[6] through the prudent use of fiscal and other incentives.

Chapter # 2 looks at the causative factors for the real estate sector being the single largest source of black money fuelled transactions. It suggests practical ways in which they can be eliminated. These are among the most crucial steps that need implementation if the excellent 2016 demonetization effort (to curb black money) is to have any real meaning. In the wake of demonetization and the subsequent Goods and Services Tax (GST) implementation, turbo charging the economy is crucial and the role of the real estate sector acquires even greater significance given its huge contributions to the national and state GDPs.

Chapters # 3 and # 4 focus on the steps that need to be taken to fight spectacular and day-to-day corruption from a practical standpoint. They also

---

[6] It is my opinion that no amount of coercion has worked in solving the income tax conundrum. Carrots, coupled with occasional sticks, rather than sticks alone will give the desired results in the long run.

look at one of the key areas of spectacular corruption—which concerns the arbitrary manner in which 'natural resource allocation' has occurred in India (in the past, especially from 2004 to 2013) to the detriment of the large majority of Indians—and suggests remedial measures to prevent the same in the future. Specifically, these chapters also suggest structural reforms with regard to fighting corruption through enactment of special acts and restructuring of institutional structures like Lokpal and Lokayuktas to make them more effective, efficient and accountable.

Chapter # 5 delves into the issue of political reform including funding of elections and political parties and suggests practical ways in which the same can be made transparent and accountable, from the perspective of the people of India. Only a vibrant democracy can, in the long run, help build a strong and resilient economy.

Chapter # 6 is the conclusion which summarizes the five key practical steps that need to be immediately implemented for the Indian economy to grow at a reasonable and excellent, if not burgeoning pace.

This apart, the chapter also focuses on the fallout of the 2016 demonetization move and its immediate consequences for the Indian people. It attempts to delineate steps that might have helped deal with the consequent snafus. It offers a historical perspective on demonetization and sheds light on the opportunities that the move could well trigger for the Indian economy.

The chapter also takes a brief look at the existing digital finance infrastructure in a bid to assess its capacity and preparedness to service growing needs. It suggests required scaling up measures, to be undertaken on priority, if there is to be a painless transition to the cashless, digital economy. It also describes the incentives and measures that would be needed to bring into the digital finance fold those people who have hitherto not been a part of the digital finance revolution.

The appendices contain relevant data and material supportive of the arguments made in the main chapters.

Chapter 1

Abolish Income Tax, Introduce a BTT and Rationalize GST

If the mythical bogeyman struck terror in our hearts while we were children, the all too real taxman strikes fear in our hearts even after we are all grown up. Not even the most honest and upright amongst us can claim to have a particular affinity for the species. The farther away they are, the greater at peace we are. And yet, their tentacles reach out and ensnare us all the time, in ways that we sometimes don't even notice. Then there are the times when we feel that we are directly under their microscopic scrutiny, like cornered organisms that lie trapped under their gaze. Either which way, there is no hope of escape.

Why such an aversion to the taxman, though, and why the desperation to get away from their scrutiny? Why do the palms of even the mightiest amongst us sweat in their presence? It is obviously because the taxman's job is to take away from us a portion of our hard earned money. Their justifications of common good simply don't convince us but we are not empowered to resist.

Wikipedia defines tax[7] (from the Latin taxo) as a financial charge or other levy imposed upon a taxpayer (an individual or legal entity) by a state or the functional equivalent of a state to fund various public expenditures. Taxation is not some novel phenomenon that came in with the advent of modern society; rather the principle dates back to ancient times.

The great Indian epic *Mahabharata* offers advice on taxation to the ruler of the day:

> "The king should take wealth from his subjects at the proper time... Like an intelligent man milking his cow every day, the king should milk his kingdom every day. As the bee collects honey from flowers gradually, without causing harm to the tree; the king should draw wealth gradually from his kingdom for storing it." — **Bhishma's counsel to Yudhishthira.** (*Mahabharata*, Book 12: Santi Parva: Rajadharmanusasana Parva)

A Sumerian tablet dating back to 2500 B.C. makes a reference[8] to payment of tax, which was rather rightly referred to as 'burden'. In ancient

---

[7] See *Charles E. McLure, Jr.* "Taxation", Britannica, Retrieved March 3, 2015— https://en.wikipedia.org/wiki/Tax
[8] See 'Taxes in the Ancient World', December 2, 2016, *University of Pennsylvania Almanac*,
http://www.upenn.edu/almanac/v48/n28/AncientTaxes.html

Mesopotamia, since coined money wasn't prevalent, ancient households paid taxes in kind, and all through the year. Merchants were required to pay tolls, duty fees and other taxes while transporting goods from one region to another. Not surprisingly, along with references to levies, there is mention of tax evasion too. The Mesopotamian merchants frequently took to smuggling to escape the tax dragnet. A letter dated around 1900 B.C. details the consequences of such evasion, as written by a trader from the head office to his employee:

> "Irra's son sent smuggled goods to Pushuken but his smuggled goods were intercepted. The Palace then threw Pushuken in jail! The guards are strong...please don't smuggle anything else!"

Clearly, people didn't enjoy paying taxes back then, just as they don't today. When more and more people find ways to evade the taxman by not bringing their income/wealth or a portion of it into the books, such unaccounted monies slowly accumulate and fuel a whole new parallel (shadow) economy that subsists alongside the formal economy. No portion of the income derived from it is contributed to state expenditure on 'common good'.

Like their counterparts in history, most governments choose tax raids and punitive justice as the weapons to be unleashed on such hoarders of cash. The Government of India chose the not so commonly used weapon of demonetization, for the third time in the last seventy years. The stated objective, of course, was to slay the demon of black money, along with lesser demons like counterfeit currency and bring to light the 'underground economy' that had remained under the spell of the 'black money' demon.

Suddenly, a whole stash of black money held in the form of Specified Bank Notes (SBNs) had ceased to be legal tender. The only hope of redemption was if it surrendered itself to the formal financial system, which would replace it with valid currency. Not all of it, though. The holders of the 'black money' would have still had to lose a significant portion of it to the much reviled taxman, much more than they would have had to if they had thought to disclose it right when it had accrued.

On the night of demonetization, Prime Minister Modi announced that a 200 percent penalty would be levied on such disclosed monies, the source of which was not explained to the satisfaction of the tax authorities. Along with the existing tax rate of 30 percent, and the additional penalty of 200 percent of the tax to be paid, the final effective rate of tax would be 90 percent. In effect, the hoarders would be left with a mere 10 percent in value of the black money they had accumulated and would find the taxman breathing down their necks possibly for perpetuity.

Just as they adopted creative ways to hide their accumulated 'black money' from the public gaze, in the form of gold, stocks and, more often, real estate, the evaders scurried around in the days following demonetization, trying their best to save as much as they could of their stashed away black money reserves. There were hurried purchases of gold with backdated bills and purchases of foreign exchange at a premium. Salaries and other dues were paid in advance and memberships of exclusive spas and gymnasiums were renewed. There were also reports that crores of rupees worth of currency was either burnt or dumped into rivers and/or garbage bins.[9]

Since it was declared that deposits under Rs 2.5 lakh the prevailing income tax exemption limit, would not attract the taxman's scrutiny, there were those who hurriedly hired money mules or used their own employees[10] to deposit the cash into their accounts in return for a commission or to get the notes exchanged across the counters at banks/post offices. The Jan Dhan accounts,[11] opened as part of the Government's drive to bring those excluded from the formal financial system within its fold, were targeted by businessmen seeking ways in which to surreptitiously convert their black money reserves.

---

[9] See 'One week after demonetisation announcement, crores of old currency notes burned, destroyed, dumped', November 16, 2016, *Business Standard*, BS Web Team, http://www.business-standard.com/article/current-affairs/demonetisation-effect-one-week-after-announcement-crores-old-currency-notes-burned-destroyed-dumped-116111600335_1.html

[10] See 'Misuse of bank account for black money deposit to invite govt action', November 18, 2016, *Hindustan Times,* Mahua Venkatesh, http://www.hindustantimes.com/india-news/misuse-of-bank-account-for-black-money-deposit-to-invite-govt-action/story-NmqcCcCsz5pmJGy2E1oHGJ.html

[11] See 'Dead since birth, Jan Dhan accounts now flush with cash', November 12, 2016, *The Economic Times,* Yogesh Dubey and Aditya Dev, http://economictimes.indiatimes.com/industry/banking/finance/banking/dead-since-birth-jan-dhan-accounts-now-flush-with-cash/articleshow/55385716.cms

There were even reports of bank staff colluding on such transactions. Touts[12] were seen offering to exchange the currency for a fee, sometimes as high as 40 percent of the value. Clearly, people were willing to lose a significant portion of the money to touts or others rather than face the wrath of the taxman. Of course, there was also the issue of expediency, since deposit/exchange of SBNs with banks involved standing for long hours in queues and would not serve their need for immediate cash.

The government soon realized the tactics that people were resorting to in a bid to avoid coming under tax scrutiny and being penalized. Limits were imposed on over the counter currency exchange and warnings were issued that *benami*[13] account deposits would come under scrutiny and face penalty.[14]

So why do people go to such extremes and risk legal action in a bid to avoid paying tax and why is the government going to such extreme measures to

---

[12] See 'A Delhi Trader Reveals How Touts Are Helping People Convert Their Black Cash Into New Notes', November 25, 2016, *Scoop Whoop*, Swati Goel Sharma, https://www.scoopwhoop.com/A-Delhi-Trader-Reveals-How-Touts-Are-Converting-Peoples-Black-Money-Into-New-Notes/#.ub4wslv3b

[13] *Benami* is a Persian language word that means "without name" or "no name". The word is used to define a transaction in which the real beneficiary is not the one in whose name the transaction has been conducted. As a result, the person in whose name the transaction is conducted is just a mask for the real beneficiary.

[14] See 'Demonetisation: Misuse of bank account for black money deposit to invite govt action', November 24, 2016, *The Indian Express*, PTI, http://indianexpress.com/article/india/india-news-india/demonetisation-government-to-prosecute-jan-dhan-account-holders-for-black-money-deposit-4382373/

ensure they cough up what is due, and even more as fines?

In the context of a developing economy like India, where large sections of the population are still in need of state intervention to gain access to basic amenities and services, public expenditure on infrastructure building is necessarily huge. This is also because of the high degree of inequity that prevails, wherein 45 percent of India's wealth is controlled by her millionaires with the figure shooting up to 54 percent if the NRI[15] millionaires are included.[16]

With such a lopsided distribution of wealth, the State's role in restoring some degree of equity assumes significance and rightfully so. To enable the majority of its citizens to gain access to resources and services that they might not be able to afford, the State has to necessarily create public infrastructure in areas like food supplies, drinking water, health, education, transport and sanitation among others, which are integral to the basic quality of life. Besides, there are other state controlled areas like power generation,[17] roads and highway building,

---

[15] A Non-Resident Indian (NRI) is a citizen of India who holds an Indian passport and has temporarily emigrated to another country for six months or more for employment, residence, education or any other purpose.

[16] This is revealed in a report of New World Wealth, a wealth research firm. See 'Yes, India has massive income inequality—but it isn't the second-most unequal country in the world', September 6, 2016, *Scroll.in,* Mayank Jain, http://scroll.in/article/815751/yes-india-has-massive-income-inequality-but-it-isnt-the-second-most-unequal-country-in-the-world

[17] Although, in the last several years, power generation and transmission has been privatized to some extent, the state can still be

communication networks, etc., that are crucial to the country's economic growth. Given that the state plays a hugely important role in the provision of some of these infrastructural services, the government undoubtedly needs to levy charges on its citizens commensurate with the usage of these services. Yet, the levies need to be heavily subsidized given that the services would be otherwise removed from the reach of the poor.

And if these subsidies are to be made possible, then the state needs to target the wealth of the rich to finance the same. That is precisely the reason why income tax slabs are created to allow for higher taxation of the economically privileged. It is on the same basis that the services availed by the well-to-do are often differentially priced, be it charges for electricity and water or additional taxes in case of property and/or wealth taxes.

Now, when large amounts of money float in the parallel or the black economy, whether in the form of cash or as assets, they are effectively monies that are being kept away from financing investment of infrastructure and services, including those for the poor. Given that a major portion of the black money is again concentrated in the hands of the wealthy, it follows that the existing inequities in the country are

---

said to be a large player in the power sector. With regard to infrastructure in general, Public Private Partnerships (PPP's) are getting to be the norm these days. However, none of these diminish the important role that the state has to play in facilitating greater quality of access to these services for the poor, marginalized and excluded populations.

being perpetuated, since these monies are most often converted to assets or splurged on conspicuous and wasteful consumption expenditure.[18] In the interests of not allowing one section of society to grow at the expense of all others, the principle of taxation that lawfully pinches the pockets of the rich to line the stomachs of the poor would seem fair and just.

Flipping sides, the same principle might not appear so fair to those who don't see the need to ensure equitable distribution. For them, their income is a product of their own efforts, possibly aided by ancestral wealth, and so they do not feel the need to share the same with someone who is not blessed with similar privilege, be it in terms of circumstances of birth or social status or skill. Wealth breeds a sense of entitlement and so, many times, the wealthy do not even understand the rationale of subsidies. They see it as a case of their rights being compromised when differential pricing is adopted on the supply of essential services like power and water, for example. Most often they do not make use of public infrastructure in areas like education, health and transportation and fail to see the rationale behind why *they* are required to contribute to the establishment or the operation of such infrastructure by levying higher taxes on their income. To put it simply, they do not see value for their money.

So they find ways to escape or short circuit the tax system, be it by under-quoting their income, undervaluing the properties they buy or sell, through

---

[18] There are many examples that can be provided here.

buying products and services without proper bills and receipts and so on.

There can be no better illustration of this 'escapist attitude' with regard to taxation than the immediate kneejerk responses that the demonetization announcement elicited, which have been detailed in my previous book.[19]

On November 29, 2016, the Taxation Laws (Second Amendment) Bill,[20] 2016, was passed in the lower house of the Indian parliament, bringing radical changes to the taxation/penalty on undisclosed income. When the demonetization announcement came, the tax[21] proposed on the unaccounted demonetized cash was close to 90 percent (tax plus penalty of 200 percent). With the amendment, it was revised to a tax of 30 percent of the income declared, a 33 percent additional surcharge on the tax amount, and a further penalty of 10 per cent of the declared income. In all, the tax liability including penalties totalled up to about 50 percent. Besides the tax component, the amendment also clarified that 25 percent of the declared income was to be deposited

---

[19] See 'The Cinderella Notes', December 2016, Shruthikka Media World, Ramesh S Arunachalam.

[20] See 'Amid disruptions & uproar, Bill to tax deposits passed in Lok Sabha', November 29, 2016, *The Hindu,* Special Correspondent, http://www.thehindu.com/news/national/Amid-disruptions-uproar-Bill-to-tax-deposits-passed-in-Lok-Sabha/article16720245.ece

[21] See 'Demonetisation: Deposits above Rs 2.5 lakh to face tax, penalty on mismatch, says Hasmukh Adhia', November 10, 2016, *ENS Economic Bureau,* The Indian Express, http://indianexpress.com/article/india/india-news-india/demonetisation-rs-500-rs-1000-deposits-above-rs-2-5-lakh-tax-penalty-on-mismatch-hasmukh-adhia-4367184/

in an interest-free deposit scheme to be notified by the government in consultation with the Reserve Bank of India (RBI). All of this was applicable provided the person concerned voluntarily disclosed it.

If, however, such unaccounted income were to be discovered subsequent to December 30, 2016, a flat tax of 60 percent, a further surcharge of 25 percent on the tax amount, and a possible 10 percent penalty at the discretion of the assessing officer would apply. The total levy on undeclared income or assets could then be as high as 85 percent.

Clearly, the intent of the government was (a good one) to try to retrieve from the economy as much as possible of the black money in circulation as cash. After all, having it thrown into fire or water did not really serve anyone's purpose.

The amendment seemed to receive a thumbs up[22] from the experts who believed that this could be an incentive for more of the defaulters to declare their unaccounted income.

It was expected that it was going to take until the end of December (2016),[23] which was when this last

---

[22] See 'Income Tax Act amendment a 'win-win', to boost govt revenues: Experts', November 28, 2016, *The Indian Express,* PTI, http://indianexpress.com/article/india/india-news-india/income-tax-act-amendment-a-win-win-to-boost-govt-revenues-experts/
[23] As per the original demonetization notification, SBNs could be deposited after the expiry of the December 30 deadline at specified RBI offices until a later date to be notified by them. But the scheme for voluntary disclosure of the income ended on December 30, 2016.

chance at voluntary disclosure was also to close, to arrive at a final figure on the total value of SBNs surrendered to the system. Figures released by the RBI indicate that, between November 10 and December 10, banks saw SBNs worth Rs 12.44 lakh crore[24] being deposited and/or exchanged. What percentage of the deposits is black money is something that would need to be ascertained[25]. The final SBNs deposited at the end of the demonetization exercise totaled Rs 15.28 lakh crore.[26]

Looking back, was the demonetization successful? While the demonetization exercise might have helped to mop up the cash component of 'black money' in circulation in the market for the time being, it was not a long-term solution to the problem. A more permanent solution would be a rationalization of the taxation system and also an attitudinal change[27] in the people apropos taxation.

So, how do we influence attitudinal change and, how do we reconcile a sense of justice with a sense of

---

See 'Withdrawal of Legal Tender Status for Rs 500 and Rs1000 Notes: RBI Notice'. November 8, 2016, RBI Press Release, https://rbi.org.in/Scripts/BS_PressReleaseDisplay.aspx?prid=38520
[24] See 'Shri R. Gandhi and Shri S. S. Mundra, RBI Deputy Governors brief Agencies on Currency Issues: Edited Transcript', December 13, 2016, *Reserve Bank of India,* Press Release,
https://rbi.org.in/Scripts/BS_PressReleaseDisplay.aspx?prid=38886
[25] Ascertaining this has not been possible in a scientific sense.
[26] See 'Finance Ministry: Demonetization immensely beneficial to Indian Economy and People', August 30, 2017, Press Information Bureau, Government of India, Ministry of Finance,
https://pib.gov.in/newsite/printrelease.aspx?relid=170378
[27] That attitudes influence behaviors goes without saying.

entitlement? For, unless this rationalization happens, black money or the parallel economy is going nowhere.

Attitudinal change requires a two-pronged approach. To begin with, you need to make the taxation system more rational and less punitive and secondly, you must make the taxpayer feel that paying taxes is worth his while. In fact, today's cash crunch in India seems to have been created through a certain loss of confidence, leading people to keep a tight hold on cash in their hand, to wait, watch and play it safe with regard to spending it. The RBI[28] has repeatedly appealed to the people not to hoard cash and has cautioned them that this would only make the situation worse. The government has also repeatedly tried to reassure[29] them of the adequacy of cash reserves.

A dip in purchasing power, even if self-imposed, has the potential to lead to an overall (at least, temporary) slowdown with the wheels of the economy juddering to a screeching halt. That is exactly what has happened, over the last three years because of demonetization (which was a well-meaning measure)

---

[28] See for example, 'Enough cash available, don't hoard, RBI tells people', November 13, 2016, *Hindustan Times*, Beena Parmar, http://www.hindustantimes.com/business-news/enough-cash-available-don-t-hoard-rbi-tells-people/story-QIJZzNN4dxYjUvBD3irZcL.html

[29] See 'Demonetisation: RBI has more than adequate cash, says Arun Jaitley', December 20, 2016, Catch News, Speed News Desk, http://www.catchnews.com/national-news/demonetisation-rbi-has-more-than-adequate-cash-says-arun-jaitley-1482222521.html

and other factors (like the near simultaneous implementation of the GST).

Anyway, looking forward, it goes without saying that India can ill-afford a slowdown at this time, right when things appear to be looking up on the economic front globally and when the economies of competitors like China are displaying sluggish tendencies. The government needs to put the confidence back in the economy, make people loosen their purse strings and go back to their spending ways. For this to happen, the government needs to give them very good news, hope for the future and put them in the mood to celebrate.

What better news can a taxpayer hope for than a tax cut to be told that he will have more discretionary income at his disposal. The immediate way forward then is a reform of the income tax structure. While it might or might not apply to the current financial year, the good news on tax cuts for the following financial year must reach their ears in double quick time. A future saving will certainly provide the right impetus and confidence for the people to give up the austere ways that demonetization has pushed them to. Income tax proposals have that kind of power over an economy, the power to make or break it.

In the long term, taxation laws need to be simplified. The taxman needs a makeover, from being the real world's bogeyman to someone who will counsel and handhold you through the process of filing your tax returns, rather than frighten you with the power of his position. Wherever and whenever possible, positive reinforcement rather than the threat of punitive action must be used to influence attitudes and bring about behavioural changes. A transparent and simple tax system can go a long way to helping people negotiate their way through it, rather than be lost in the quagmire that it is presently.

Taxation should be *pareto optimal*—it should neither diminish the drive for enterprise nor should it result in huge inequities due to the hoarding of money by a select few. An unduly high tax rate and low exemption limits are constraining factors on consumption and enterprise. That is why having a transparent and forward looking tax system is critical for any economy.

What are the criteria that enable a system to be a forward looking transparent tax system?

First: **simplicity.**
Second: **transaction cost.**
Third: **ease of implementation.**
Fourth: **openness.**
Fifth: **equitability.**

Students of accounting and commerce often complain about the difficulty in clearing their Income Tax exams, such is the level of complexity in interpretation and application of the rules that frame the system. There is often disagreement even amongst audit professionals over exemptions, limits and deductions. No wonder then that the common man feels highly pressurized through the process of filing his tax returns. Starting February through July, the salaried classes have a haunted look about them as they grapple with the demons of tax returns. If they already feel the pinch of having to pay a tax, which they feel is not entirely fair, the complexity of the process only adds further aggravation.

The complexity of the task directly feeds into transaction cost as the amount of time, effort and resources that the tax filing process demands is inversely proportional to the benefits that the taxpayers feel they derive from the process.

The complex nature of the taxation process demands considerable time and resources from the system itself in order for the tax laws to be effectively implemented. If the structural issues are an impediment to the ease of implementation, the rather dated tools available to the taxman are another big problem. Although the methods used to identify potential defaulters have been updated in terms of technology, their inclusion in data gathering continues to remain a work-in-progress.

The element of secrecy associated with the process is yet another issue, although it is possibly linked to the threat of punitive force that is used to ensure compliance and of course, to the felt need to evade the process to whatever degree possible. There is a shroud of secrecy confining the process and the implementation, and the taxman is this mysterious figure one is always fearing and constantly trying to second guess.

While India has achieved much in its income tax proposals from the 1970s, there is still a lot more left to be done. Most budgets tend to address the issue superficially, more in terms of exemption limits and tax rates. Not much thought is given to simplifying the procedures and processes involved in making it less of a cumbersome, unpleasant chore. Furthermore, tax reforms need to address both the complex process of filing tax returns and also the tax rates applicable to different income slabs.

A pre-requisite for tax reform suggestions is a thorough and complete understanding of the existing systems and processes. Furthermore, the magnitude of impact that is likely to occur needs to be understood, given the quantum of resources generated as taxes.

A look at the estimates of income tax revenue of the government should give us a fair idea of the kind of monies accrued. The revenue from direct taxes for the FY 2018-2019 stood at Rs 11.37 lakh crore as shown in appendix 1. The direct tax revenue as a percentage of gross tax revenues stood at a little over 54.78 percent in FY 2018-2019. Any proposal to revise the direct taxes is hence bound to have a significant impact on the country's tax revenues and this needs to be kept in mind.

The Nagpur based economic think-tank Arthakranti,[30] which has reportedly claimed credit for

---

[30] See 'Banking Transaction Tax: After demonetisation, Arthakranti wants Narendra Modi to abolish Income Tax', November 18, 2016, *Artha Kranti,* India.com, http://www.arthakranti.org/news-events/238-banking-transaction-tax-after-demonetisation-arthakranti-wants-narendra-modi-to-abolish-income-tax

proposing the idea of demonetization to Prime Minister Modi, has proposed a complete abolition of all direct and indirect taxes levied by the Union Government, the various state governments and all local bodies across the country, with the exception of customs and import duties that function as international trade balancers. Instead, they propose a Banking Transactions Tax (BTT) at the rate of 2 percent on all banking transactions, with the exception of cash withdrawals.

Given that demonetization was expected to bring a large number of the as yet excluded population into the formal banking system, the belief that the accruals from the banking transactions tax would compensate for the loss of income tax collections given the increased volume of transactions seems reasonable. Without doubt, an abolition of income tax would come as a big relief to the individual taxpayers, who would be left with a much larger discretionary income at their disposal and hence much improved purchasing power. This in turn will give a much needed push to economic activity and growth. That is the supreme logic behind the introduction of the BTT and removal of direct taxes.

Banking transactions tax[31] as a concept is not new to the Indian fiscal system. The tax was introduced in

---

[31] See 'Govt abolishes banking transaction tax', April 1, 2009, *The Indian Express,* Agencies,
http://indianexpress.com/article/business/banking-and-finance/govt-abolishes-banking-transaction-tax/

2005 by the earlier (UPA[32]) regime as a mechanism to trace black money. It was levied only on cash withdrawals of greater than Rs 50,000 (for individuals) and Rs 1,00,000 (for others) in a single working day from the non-savings accounts maintained with scheduled banks. The tax was subsequently withdrawn in 2009.

Given that BTT would be a flat, single-point tax to be levied by commercial banks on all bank transactions, it would be simple to implement and have practically zero compliance cost. With the numbers of those within the fold of the banking system expected to increase significantly (given the drive for 100 percent financial inclusion), BTT is likely to generate the required tax revenue and have buoyancy besides. The negative fallout might be an attempt at bypassing the banking system, but certain additional measures need to be undertaken to ensure that people prefer not to transact in cash, wherever and whenever possible. However, there exists the challenge of ensuring that the people newly entering the banking system remain within its fold. Simplifying banking procedures and improving the quality of and access to other support services[33] should help achieve that.

Coming back to the BTT, let us look at transaction numbers to understand how beneficial the BTT could be if implemented. For example, for the FY 2018-19 alone, the total value of RBI payment system

---

[32] UPA stands for United Progressive Alliance. See https://en.wikipedia.org/wiki/United_Progressive_Alliance
[33] Please see appendix 1c for some ideas on the same.

transactions stood at Rs 28,86,465 billion,[34] which is 28,86,46,500 crore (as 1 billion Rs = Rs 100 crore).

If we compute a BTT of Rs 0.75 per Rs 100 across this 28,86,46,500 crore that flowed through the RBI payment system in FY 2018-19, we get a BTT collection of Rs 28,86,46,500 crore multiplied by 0.75 and then, divided by 100. This equals Rs 21,64,849 crore. Thus, if one were to try to make a projection based on the total BTT estimate using RBI payment system data for FY 2018-19, the annual total yield from BTT would have been able to easily compensate for the loss of revenue from all direct and indirect taxes which stood at Rs 20,76,703 crore as per estimates available from the Central Board of Direct Taxes (CBDT) given in appendix 1. And more importantly, it would have been far easier and less costly to implement and ensure compliance.

That said, while on the subject of tax reforms as a means to combat black money, the issue of unaccounted income stashed away in offshore accounts needs to be considered as well. Indeed, many of the opponents to the 2016 demonetization move have criticized it on the grounds that it attempted to address only the negligible cash component of the black money in circulation within the country, while turning a blind eye to the black money converted to assets like real estate, gold or stock and most importantly, cash deposits in offshore accounts.

---

[34] Please see appendix 1a.

Given that real estate constitutes about a tenth of the Indian economy, the black money floating around in real estate is estimated to be many times higher[35] than the riches stashed away in offshore accounts. One can only hope that rationalization of taxes on the acquisition of property, and also personal income tax and corporate tax rates, will prove a natural deterrent to the real estate sector continuing to be the receptacle of black money that it currently is. The next chapter deals with the issue of real estate in a complete and comprehensive manner.

On the matter of repatriating black money lying in offshore accounts, the government is faced with a formidable task and significant legal wrangling given that it also involves the framework of the prevailing laws of those countries where the monies lie.

According to a Bank of Italy estimate, Indians[36] were said to have stashed away $152-$181 billion in offshore foreign bank accounts. Recent estimates[37] have, however, pegged the same as between $216-$500 billion in offshore bank accounts. Although

---

[35] See 'Real estate: An industry built on black money', December 5, 2014, *Rediff.com,* Bhupesh Bhandari,
http://www.rediff.com/money/report/pix-column-real-estate-an-industry-built-on-black-money/20141205.htm

[36] See 'Baiting the big fish', October 6, 2016, *India Today,* Shweta Punj, http://indiatoday.intoday.in/story/black-money-tax-income-tax-modi-government-income-disclosure-scheme/1/781362.html

[37] See 'Indians' unaccounted wealth abroad estimated at $216-490 billion: Studies', June 24, 2019, PTI, https://economictimes.indiatimes.com/news/economy/finance/indians-unaccounted-wealth-abroad-estimated-at-216-490-billion-studies/articleshow/69928218.cms?from=mdr and Wikipedia https://en.wikipedia.org/wiki/Indian_black_money

India has had to depend on revelations like the Panama Papers exposé until now for access to data, the country has signed agreements with several OECD[38] member countries for automatic flow of information, which came into effect from January, 2017. Swiss banks[39] have also agreed to share information on Indian account holders from September, 2019, following a joint declaration signed between the two countries. A revised tax treaty has also been signed with Mauritius[40] to enable the government to tax capital gains on investments routed through the island nation, one of the preferred tax havens of Indian investors. India has signed a DTAA (Double Taxation Avoidance Agreement)[41] with 88 countries, including most major countries such as the United States, the United Kingdom, Australia and France. Mauritius, Cyprus and Singapore were the only three countries where the agreement was earlier not in force. As of 2016,

---

[38] The Organisation for Economic Co-operation and Development (OECD) (French: *Organisation de coopération et de développement économiques, OCDE*) is an intergovernmental economic organisation with 35 member countries, founded in 1961 to stimulate economic progress and world trade.

[39] See 'Swiss Banks to share info on Indian A/C holders', November 22, 2016, *The Times of India*, PTI,
http://timesofindia.indiatimes.com/india/Swiss-Banks-to-share-info-on-Indian-A/C-holders-from-Sept-2019/articleshow/55562640.cms

[40] See 'Revised Indo-Mauritius tax treaty to curb tax evasion: Finance Ministry', August 29, 2016, *The Economic Times*, PTI,
http://economictimes.indiatimes.com/news/economy/policy/revised-indo-mauritius-tax-treaty-to-curb-tax-evasion-finance-ministry/articleshow/53912921.cms

[41] See 'All you wanted to know about...DTAA', May 16, 2016, The Hindu Business Line, Parvatha Vardhini.C,
http://www.thehindubusinessline.com/opinion/columns/all-you-wanted-to-know-aboutdtaa/article8607732.ece

the agreements with both Mauritius and Cyprus have been renegotiated and signed, while it is hoped that the treaty with Singapore[42] will be signed before the end of the fiscal period. All of these come as huge jolts to Indian investors hoping to avoid paying tax on income from capital gains.

The provisions of the Prevention of Money Laundering Act[43] (PMLA) and FEMA[44] (Foreign Exchange Management Act) were amended under the Undisclosed Foreign Income and Assets (Imposition of Tax) Bill,[45] 2015, to ensure that, in the event of undisclosed assets held by a person abroad not being attachable, assets of equivalent value held by such a person in India would be confiscated. The bill proposed that a flat tax rate of 30 percent, without allowing for any of the exemptions permitted under the Income Tax Act would be applied on all foreign income.

An enhanced punishment including imprisonment for between 3-10 years and a penalty of three times

---

[42] See 'India hopeful of signing new tax treaty with Singapore by this fiscal end', May 16, 2016, *The Hindu Business Line,* Surabhi, http://www.thehindubusinessline.com/economy/policy/india-hopeful-of-signing-new-tax-treaty-with-singapore-by-this-fiscal-end/article8607967.ece

[43] See 'Prevention of Money Laundering Act, 2002', http://finmin.nic.in/law/moneylaunderingact.pdf

[44] See 'Foreign Exchange Management Act, 1999', Income Tax Department, http://www.incometaxindia.gov.in/pages/acts/foreign-exchange-management-act.aspx

[45] See 'The Undisclosed Foreign Income and Assets (Imposition of Tax) Bill, 2015', as introduced in the Lok Sabha, http://www.incometaxindia.gov.in/Documents/Undisclosed-Foreign-Income-Bill-2015.pdf

the tax amount, amounting to 90 percent of the undisclosed income was also proposed on any wilful non-disclosure or tax evasion. A one-time compliance window was also announced between June and September, 2015, for Indian citizens to declare information on all previously undisclosed assets, which would be taxed at a flat 30 percent along with a penalty of 100 percent of the tax amount. The rate of taxation in effect was 60 percent of the undisclosed income. During the compliance period, the disclosures would not attract the provisions of FEMA or PMLA.

The scheme was not particularly successful, netting only Rs 3,770 crore[46] in income disclosures with a 60 percent tax plus penalty to be levied on them. The figure cannot reflect more than a miniscule portion of the cash and assets held abroad.

Clearly, there is a need for better incentives if the country is to be successful in repatriating funds and assets from abroad. While the law has been sufficiently armed to prosecute them, it will only end up being a long drawn out process and might not yield the results hoped for. Instead, if compliance can be achieved voluntarily, by providing sufficient incentives for the offenders to disclose their foreign holdings and bring them back to the country, it would do the economy far greater good. Rather than imposing heavy penalties, we need to encourage the

---

[46] See 'Why black money scheme was a superflop, and what Modi can do to redeem it', October 3, 2015, *First Post,* R Jagannathan, http://www.firstpost.com/business/why-the-black-money-scheme-was-a-superflop-and-what-modi-can-do-to-redeem-it-2452626.html

individual to disclose his assets with minimal penalties as opposed to completely losing the use of them in the form of stiff penalties.

Yet another reform that has been discussed is the adoption of a something similar to the American IRS (Internal Revenue Service) scheme. The success of the IRS in attracting foreign capital of Americans (back) into the United States needs commendation.

The system basically allows a country to tax the income and wealth of all its citizens, irrespective of where it originates from. Once again, issues such as transparency and sharing of data and information are crucial to the success of such a measure.

The larger point to be underlined here is that the stick alone cannot work, carrots are needed too and they must be sufficiently designed so that they encourage the return of foreign capital back to India in a voluntary manner. Engaging in legal battles with institutions in overseas countries can become counter productive and a waste of time and money.

Overall, the restructuring of the tax system should be made attractive enough to the taxpayer to want to retain his capital within the country, rather than go to the trouble of transferring and maintaining it in offshore accounts.

Apart from structural reforms, compliance windows and simplifying tax procedures, the other critical aspect that needs addressing, with respect to influencing attitudinal change, is the cost benefit analysis to the taxpayer. By benefit, I do not refer to personal benefit alone but benefit to the larger society. If the taxpayer sees the tax he pays yield dividend in the form of better public health, education, transport and other infrastructure, he might start feeling more invested in the process of nation building. If, however, he perceives no change in the quality of public infrastructure and sees the bulk of his tax money going towards wasteful and extravagant government expenditure, he would feel increasingly resentful of the taxation process.

It is, therefore, imperative to trim the fat from government expenditure, to make it a mean and lean machine that delivers true cost benefits to the exchequer. After having willingly borne the pain of demonetization in 2016, the taxpayer will certainly want to see the lawmakers and bureaucrats responding by practicing a certain austerity in the use of public money and diverting all public resources to projects intended for public good.

Also, it is imperative that the government machinery starts recognizing that it is accountable to the taxpayer, whose tax money is what keeps it lubricated and running. The attitude of policy makers, bureaucrats and other government staff also needs to change towards the taxpayer and he needs to be accorded the respect he deserves in his interactions with the State. He must not be pushed around or trifled with and he must not be expected to pay bribes and commissions to get work done within the government. It would be adding insult to injury if, after willingly participating in the war against corruption and black money, he is forced to bribe his way through the government's administrative labyrinth to get his license, permits or even his pension/dues—all this even after following due process.

From posing a conundrum, the taxation system needs to evolve into a more just, compassionate and simple process that the taxpayer is happily willing to participate in, simply because he perceives a palpable difference on the ground that convinces him that there is a point to it after all, one of larger good!

Accordingly, the following changes to the present direct tax system are suggested:

a) A crucial step here is to abolish all direct taxes— i.e. personal income tax and corporate tax including all kinds of capital gains tax (both short and long term). Corporate tax will also be abolished for all body corporates including trusts, societies and the like. The same will be substituted with a banking transaction tax (BTT) of 75 paise per every Rs 100. Based on FY 2018-19 data, this BTT would have facilitated revenue collection[47] to the tune of Rs 21.65 lakh crore[48] as against a direct tax collection of Rs 11.37 lakh crore.

---

[47] See appendix 1 and 1a.
[48] For FY 2018-19, the total value of RBI payment system transactions stood at Rs 28,86,465 billion, which is Rs 28,86,46,500 crore (1 billion Rs = Rs 100 crore). If we compute a BTT of Rs 0.75 per Rs 100 across this Rs 28,86,46,500 crore flowing through the payment system, we get a BTT collection of Rs (28,86,46,500 crore x 0.75)/100 which equals Rs 21,64,849 crore or Rs 21.65 lakh crore.

As the velocity of the banking transactions increase, the BTT would also be good enough to cover any potential deficits in the indirect taxes (whose reform is given below) and perhaps even help in eliminating these totally as well. The BTT should ultimately settle down at 50 paise per Rs 100, once the system stabilizes. The BTT is what I see as a fair system to taxation, without burdening the common person—it will bring into its fold, almost everyone in the country from a tax perspective. Currently, less than 10 percent of India is part of the direct tax system.

b) Another crucial step is to demonetize the following currency—Rs 2,000, Rs 500, Rs 200 and Rs 100. Meanwhile, prior preparation is required to step up digital capacity in the country in terms of more ATMs and enhance effectiveness of the cash management system in existing ATMs. Furthermore, there are many low income people who lack the digital and process literacy to be seamlessly integrated into the transforming, digitally oriented economy. They have to be assisted significantly so that they are not left behind. The various key measures required to achieve this are outlined in appendix 1c.

Money supply must also be significantly enhanced in terms of new Rs 200, Rs 100 and Rs 50 notes. This implies that large currency will be done away with altogether. All logistics must be worked out properly to avoid the problems faced in the demonetization exercise of 2016. The demonetized currency can be used for emergency services with a logistically managed cut-off date—this is to ensure that there is no hardship for the people at large.

c) People must be given 120 days to deposit all of their cash held in the form of the above currencies (that would have ceased to be legal tender as on the date of demonetization, barring the exception of use for emergency services immediately). **Likewise, all people with illegal deposits in banks abroad would also be able to bring in their money as long as pay a BTT of Rs 10 per Rs 100.** It is estimated[49] that between $216-$500 billion of illegal Indian money lies abroad in overseas bank accounts. Assuming the actual is at least mid-point, we can reasonably peg the volume of illegal foreign money at a conservative $300 billion.

No questions are to be asked regarding the source of money as long as the cash is deposited in the bank or money is transferred to the bank from overseas. A BTT of 75 paise for every Rs 100 would be charged on all cash deposits within India (post demonetization) and Rs 10 per Rs 100 would be charged on all illegal foreign inward

---

[49] See 'Indians' unaccounted wealth abroad estimated at $216-490 billion: Studies', June 24, 2019, PTI, https://economictimes.indiatimes.com/news/economy/finance/indians-unaccounted-wealth-abroad-estimated-at-216-490-billion-studies/articleshow/69928218.cms?from=mdr and Wikipedia https://en.wikipedia.org/wiki/Indian_black_money

remittances.[50] After the illegal foreign inward remittances have come in and been lodged in the bank account (subject to a BTT of Rs 10 per Rs 100 for the first time), subsequent transactions will attract a BTT of Rs 75 paise for every Rs 100.

Thus, all rotating funds in the payment system (as defined by the RBI) will be subject to a BTT of 75 paise for every Rs 100. While cash deposits would attract a BTT of 75 paise per Rs 100, cash withdrawals would attract a BTT of Rs 1.25 per Rs 100, beyond a limit of Rs 30 lakh per quarter. Otherwise, cash withdrawals will entail a BTT of 75 paise per Rs 100. When transfers between two accounts owned by the same person occur, BTT would be 50 paise per Rs 100. Other account transfers within a family would incur a BTT of 60 paise per Rs 100. All other account transfers would attract a BTT of 75 paise per Rs 100. Current account transfers would have a BTT of Rs 1 per Rs 100.

d) While income tax would have been abolished, income, property/assets (including shares) and jewellery status returns would have to be filed at the end of the 120 days (after the demonetization exercise) so that any future sales of assets can be ensured to be through the bank only. Also, the

---

[50] As noted above, assuming that $ 300 billion of Indian illegal money lies abroad and given a BTT of Rs 10 on Rs 100, we can expect a total onetime revenue inflow of Rs 2.03 lakh crore, which can serve as the core corpus for state funding of elections discussed later.

veracity of income sources to prevent future accumulation of black money can be ensured.

e) The income tax department can be downsized and rationalized in terms of work and functions as required by the above. Redeployment of staff in other suitable departments and positions would also need to be done.

f) Anyone found contravening the spirit and character of this genuinely positive and forward looking measure will face prosecution and severe action provided they are found: (i) to have the demonetized notes after the 120-day period; and (ii) to be hoarding legal currency, beyond the prescribed limit of Rs 10 lakhs per quarter.

This means that, at most, at any time, this is the maximum permissible amount that can be found with any person/entity, subject to the condition that the quarterly cash withdrawals don't exceed Rs 30 lakhs.

Furthermore, the following reforms will be required with regard to The Goods and Services Tax (GST)[51] system. This is very necessary to put India firmly on the double digit growth path. Several steps are required in this regard:

---

[51] See 'Goods and Services Tax (GST) Bill, explained', October 19, 2016, The Indian Express, Express News Service, http://indianexpress.com/article/explained/gst-bill-parliament-what-is-goods-services-tax-economy-explained-2950335/

a) Reconstitute the GST council with sufficient representation for the civil society. Again, as in the case of the Lokpal and the Lokayuktas, the GST council must also be governed by a comprehensive conflict of interest rules to prevent corruption. The GST council must also reflect enhanced sensitivity to all kinds of MSMEs, agro enterprises and the like.

b) Rationalize the GST list, exempt essential items and implement a single national rate of 5 percent. This can be done by the reconstituted GST council.

c) Simplify compliances and reduce them to a minimal. Use value engineering to optimize the filing of GST returns and compliances, which should ideally be one form per month.

d) The reforms in direct taxes and associated processes and BTT should ensure fool proof collection of the GST via the banking channels as the scope for black transactions would have been completely eliminated. Additionally, the BTT as well as the high velocity of rotation of money through the banks (which should further enhance the BTT), should offset any potential loss in collection of the GST from previous levels[52].

---

[52] Based on FY 2018-19 data, the proposed BTT of Rs 0.75 per Rs 100 would have facilitated revenue collection to the tune of Rs 21.65 lakh crore as against a direct tax collection of Rs 11.37 lakh crore. In fact, the BTT collection, as stated above, would be more than sufficient to compensate fully for the total of indirect taxes as well which totaled Rs 9.39 lakh crore in FY 2018-19.

Also, with burgeoning growth of economy, GST, in reality, should reach record collections.

e) Completely exempt exports from purview of GST. Streamline filings and permissions in this regard. Again returns should be one page at the most.

f) A final key issue in the implementation of the GST framework is the distribution of GST revenue to the states. There is a long lead time before this money reaches the states. This has to change and an amendment introduced so that any GST accrual to the states reaches them, with a lag time of two weeks (at the maximum).

Taken together, the direct and indirect tax proposals should turbo-charge domestic consumption, enhance domestic savings, reduce interest rates for lending and make exports competitive, apart from helping to generate funds for development including infrastructure, enhance investment and transform India into a rapidly growing economy. They will also enhance the size of the economy, especially given that the parallel (black) economy and informal sector would have been fully absorbed into the mainstream. Under these circumstances, in the medium term, growth rates are expected to exceed 15 percent and this is genuinely feasible and possible. Having said that, let us now turn our attention to a critical sector in the economy—i.e., the real estate sector—and see what reforms are immediately needed there to bolster and turbocharge the economy.

Chapter 2

Reduce Stamp Duty on Property and Revise Property Guideline Values

The best investment on earth is earth
— *Louis Glickman*

Real estate is considered the best and safest of all investment options known to man. While cash or gold run the risk of thievery, investments like stocks and shares are subject to violent market fluctuations, and yet others like livestock or any other kind of perishables cannot stand the test of perpetuity. In comparison, real estate is considered the most solid of investments given its perpetual quality, likely incremental value and the marginal chances of loss by theft. While it is also subject to and likely to be impacted by the vagaries of the market, it is nowhere near as volatile, for example, as stocks/shares.

It is these very qualities of real estate that make it so sought after and even fought over. History is replete with instances of wars fought over territory or land and in the modern day context too, there are enough instances of courtroom battles over rights to property. The English philosopher John Locke described the right to property as an inalienable right and said that it was the duty of the state to secure this right for the individual.

Just as it is the world over, the desire to own property is a significant driving force for the majority of the Indian population; a piece of land or a heap of bricks that he can call his own. In the pre-independence era, the zamindars,[53] the landowners, wielded great political and economic power over the peasantry who tilled their land. With the freedom movement gaining ground in the country, there was opposition to the oppression of the zamindars and the concentration of power and wealth in the hands of a few. One of the first agrarian reforms immediately after independence was the abolition of the zamindari system through legislation enacted by the various Indian provinces. However, the Indian

---

[53] A zamindar in the Indian subcontinent was an aristocrat, typically hereditary, holding enormous tracts of land, and held control over his peasants, from whom the zamindars reserved the right to collect tax, often for military purposes.

Constitution, which came into effect on January 26, 1950, held the right to property as a fundamental right under Articles 19 and 31.[54] With this, all the previous legislations enacted by the provinces on the zamindari system were rendered constitutionally invalid. It took the first constitutional amendment in 1951 to validate the state acts and by 1956, the zamindari system had finally been abolished in many Indian provinces.

Although abolished in a legal sense, the degree of power and social status that land ownership invests in an individual cannot be wished away even today. Hence, a deeply entrenched desire to own property remains with every individual and it is their most prized possession.

Just as their fascination for the yellow metal makes Indians the world's largest consumers of gold,[55] the

---

[54] "The provisions relating to the right to property were changed a number of times. The 44th Amendment of 1978 removed the right to property from the list of fundamental rights. A new provision, Article 300-A, was added to the constitution, which provided that "no person shall be deprived of his property save by authority of law". Thus, if a legislator makes a law depriving a person of his property, there would be no obligation on the part of the state to pay anything as compensation. The aggrieved person shall have no right to move the court under Article 32. Thus, the right to property is no longer a fundamental right, though it is still a constitutional right. If the government appears to have acted unfairly, the action can be challenged in a court of law by aggrieved citizens." See 'Fundamental rights in India', Wikipedia, https://en.wikipedia.org/wiki/Fundamental_rights_in_India

[55] See 'India overtakes China, becomes biggest gold consumer: Survey', October 27, 2015, *The Economic Times*, PTI, http://economictimes.indiatimes.com/news/economy/indicators/in

significant influence that the real estate sector wields over the Indian economy can be seen from the fact that prior to the 2016 demonetization[56] it was the second largest employer[57] in the country after agriculture, and it contributed to 7 percent of the country's GDP. The Indian real estate market is projected to touch $180 billion[58] by the year 2020. The construction industry ranks third among the 14 major sectors in terms of direct, indirect and induced effects in all sectors of the economy.

While the real estate sector can boast of all these milestones, yet another achievement that might not be so flaunt-worthy is the sector's status as possibly the largest receptacle of black money in India. An Ambit Capital Research study[59] claims that black money funds around 30 percent of India's real estate sector.[60] Unlike the case of gold or stock, though,

---

dia-overtakes-china-becomes-biggest-gold-consumer-survey/articleshow/49556979.cms

[56] I am using the 2016 demonetization as a benchmark because the real estate sector has been in significant turmoil after that.

[57] See 'Demonetization: 'Housing prices already at lowest, no scope for correction,' says CREDAI', November 27, 2016, Daily News and Analysis (DNA), PTI, http://www.dnaindia.com/money/report-demonetization-housing-prices-already-at-lowest-no-scope-for-correction-says-credai-2277276

[58] See 'Real Estate Industry in India', July, 2016, *India Brand Equity Foundation (IBEF)*,
http://www.ibef.org/industry/real-estate-india.aspx

[59] See '30% of India's real estate sector funded by black money', June 6, 2016, *The Economic Times Realty*, PTI,
http://realty.economictimes.indiatimes.com/news/industry/30-of-indias-real-estate-sector-funded-by-black-money/52614378

[60] In my opinion, this is a very conservative estimate and black money should be funding at least 67 percent of the real estate sector. I base this on my grassroots experience in over 640 districts of India where I have witnessed systematic under valuing of properties based

there is no visible evidence or paper trail to establish the same. No wonder then that it is the most favored option by hoarders who wish to invest their unaccounted for cash in an asset that can offer them stability, durability and value for money leaving hardly any trace of evidence. Just as the honest citizen wants to safeguard his hard earned, tax deducted income and savings by investing in real estate, the hoarder/black marketeer too wants to hoard his cash without worrying about storage or theft or, just as importantly, detection by the taxman. In the event of tax raids, while currency bundles and jewellery can be seized on the spot and taken into possession by the officials, real estate holdings are not so easily seized. Establishing the connection between unaccounted for income or black money and the acquisition/sale of property is no easy task, and a considerable amount of legal wrangling will have to precede any move to attach real estate properties to an income tax dispute.

The Ambit study also indicated that the present government had been moving aggressively in conducting checks around gold transactions and it has become increasingly difficult to park unaccounted cash in the form of jewellery or bullion. Towards the end of 2015, the Government of India made it mandatory for the PAN[61] number to be

---

on the property guideline value. Property is rarely registered at the prevailing market rates.

[61] Permanent Account Number (PAN) is a ten-digit alphanumeric number, issued in the form of a laminated card, by the Income Tax Department in India, to any "person" who applies for it or to whom the department allots the number without an application.

quoted for all transactions in excess of Rs 2 lakh[62] from January 1, 2016. The earlier limit had been Rs 5 lakh but the government believed that the lowering of the limit was warranted because of the rampant investing of black money in gold.

The All India Gems and Jewellery Trade Federation[63] expressed great dissatisfaction over the move. They believed that it would discriminate against those people who might not have PAN cards, for a variety of legitimate reasons. Jewellers in the country even went on strike in the first week of March, 2016 over the issue of the gold tax and also over the compulsory disclosure of PAN numbers. As expected, the sale of jewellery took a hit[64] in the first half of 2016, possibly because people preferred not to leave an official trail. Disclosing one's PAN number would mean an official record of the transaction. It was also possible that some people who'd previously invested in gold were now handicapped by the lack of a PAN Card. This could be because of legitimate reasons, like in the case of

---

[62] See 'PAN made mandatory for all transactions above Rs2 lakh', December 18, 2015, *Livemint,* Remya Nair,
http://www.livemint.com/Politics/UkFNyKXvjG8oE3QxzSM6bI/PAN-compulsory-for-opening-all-bank-accountsm-says-revenue.html
[63] See 'Jewellers unhappy over mandatory PAN on purchase of Rs 2 lakh' December 16, 2015, *The Economic Times,* PTI,
http://economictimes.indiatimes.com/wealth/personal-finance-news/jewellers-unhappy-over-mandatory-pan-on-purchase-of-rs-2-lakh/articleshow/50207202.cms
[64] See 'Jewellery industry hit by mandatory PAN Card for purchases over Rs 2 lakh', June 13, 2016, *Business Standard,* Gireesh Babu,
http://www.business-standard.com/article/companies/jewellery-industry-hit-by-mandatory-pan-card-for-purchases-over-rs-2-lakh-116061300696_1.html

those with incomes that fall below the exemption limit or within the exempted category like, for example, agricultural income. The organized jewellery sector took a 50 percent hit in sales, a rather high percentage even after accounting for those without PAN cards.

Likewise, stock market transactions also appeared to have been caught in the glare of scrutiny by the taxmen. A report[65] in the *DNA* newspaper revealed that the Income Tax (I-T) department was preparing to swoop down on stock market players following a probe revealing that alleged tax evaders were parking money in companies listed on the BSE[66] in order to avoid paying tax and shroud alleged black money. The IT department had collated information on the alleged dealings of individuals and companies through the securities transaction tax (STT) data submitted by NSE[67] and BSE for 2013-14 and 2014-15. According to reports of the IT department, during 2014-15, trading of more than Rs 4,000 crore on BSE and nearly Rs 1,000 crore on NSE took place with the use of duplicate or bogus PAN card numbers. Such allegedly fraudulent dealings had only benefited the stock market. The IT department's figures for 2014-15 show that the stock market's turnover more than doubled, from Rs 32 lakh crore to Rs 66 lakh crore. In the same period, the number

---

[65] See 'IT dept to swoop down on tax evaders in stock market', October 13, 2016, *Daily News and Analysis (DNA)*, Dipu Rai, http://www.dnaindia.com/money/report-rs-30-lakh-crore-black-money-in-stock-markets-i-t-2263647
[66] Bombay Stock Exchange.
[67] National Stock Exchange of India.

of alleged and potential tax evaders soared by about 150 percent. Documents in the DNA newspaper's possession revealed that investors had routed about Rs 30 lakh crore of funds through stock transactions in a year without disclosing their income sources.

All of this effectively meant that people, looking to invest unaccounted money, found physical assets a safer option than financial assets. For example, private equity money to the extent of $1.3 billion[68] flowed into the real estate sector in the half year ending June, 2015. There is a strong possibility that a significant percentage of this is black money stashed away in offshore accounts that has now been routed back into the country in the form of foreign private equity. Despite the real estate sector struggling over the last couple years prior to demonetization,[69] there has been no dearth in the flow of private equity, with a 40 percent rise[70] at Rs 3,840 crore in the first quarter of 2016. This adds to the suspicion that a significant portion of illegal domestic money is held in the form of real estate.

---

[68] See 'Why Jaitley's threats won't work: All black money is in stock markets & real estate, too risky to touch', October 5, 2015, *Firstpost,* R Jagannathan, http://www.firstpost.com/business/why-jaitleys-threats-will-not-work-all-black-money-is-in-stock-markets-real-estate-too-risky-to-touch-2454746.html

[69] I am using the 2016 demonetization as a benchmark because the real estate sector has been in significant turmoil after that.

[70] See 'Private equity investments in realty rise 40 percent to Rs 3,840 crore in March quarter', May 7, 2016, *The Economic Times,* Ravi Teja Sharma, http://economictimes.indiatimes.com/wealth/real-estate/private-equity-investments-in-realty-rise-40-per-cent-to-rs-3840-crore-in-march-quarter/articleshow/52159685.cms

The primary criticism against demonetization was that the government was focused on flushing out the relatively small volume of the black money in circulation in the form of cash, while turning a blind eye to the reserves locked up in real estate or in offshore accounts. Going by a Finance Ministry report in 2012, real estate is said to account for almost 50 percent[71] of the black money market.

The real estate sector has a certain opacity factor that allows black money invested within to remain hidden, even while in plain sight. What this essentially means is that even while the black money is manifested in the form of the asset, making for a significant portion of its market value in fact, it remains invisible in terms of the property 'document' value.

The scope for undervaluing property in official documentation is what makes real estate the most sought after choice of the black money hoarders. The property guideline values in the land revenue registers of the revenue authorities are outdated and have not been aligned with market values in many years. So, people can easily get away with registering properties at a fraction of the market value, with only the guideline value, reflected in the property sale deed,[72]

---

[71] See 'The Un-real Estate: The sector that is going to take the biggest hit', November 13, 2016, *The Indian Express,* Smita Nair, http://indianexpress.com/article/india/india-news-india/the-un-real-estate-demonetisation-process-100-500-rupee-note-narendra-modi-black-money-4372286/
[72] This is typically the guideline value set by the state government.

being settled through a banking transaction—the remaining is usually paid in the form of black money.

While real estate deals are indeed a preferred means to camouflage unaccounted cash reserves by converting them to a fixed asset, the physical cash merely changes hands. The velocity of money then comes into play as it passes numerous hands in its travel through the economy, multiplying manifold the levels of tax evasion. More often than not, the cash component of a real estate deal is higher than the property 'document' value that is settled through a banking transaction.

In the wake of demonetization, it was believed that the real estate sector would take a huge hit given that all accumulated cash reserves of black money, in the form of high value currencies, had been rendered non-fungible. Propequity, an online subscription based real estate data and analytics platform, predicted a fall of up to 30 percent[73] in housing prices and a loss to the sector to the tune of Rs 8 lakh crore in the year, post demonetization. However, opinion is divided on that with some others feeling that no drastic fall is possible given that property prices in key markets have remained stagnant due to a three-year slowdown in the real estate sector.[74] All said and done, it has however not

---

[73] See 'Demonetisation: Housing prices to drop up to 30%, wiping Rs 8 lakh cr in value', November 24, 2016, *Firstpost*, PTI,
http://www.firstpost.com/business/demonetisation-housing-prices-to-drop-up-to-30-wiping-rs-8-lakh-cr-in-value-3122946.html
[74] See 'Opinion divided over impact of demonetisation on real estate prices', November 21, 2016, *Livemint*, Bidya Sapam,
http://www.livemint.com/Companies/o2fVwCBoD8rrJv12XaENm

been possible to ascertain any of this with certainty given the lack of reliable and valid data with regard to the real estate sector, especially because of the huge black money component that still exists in real estate transactions, even as of today.

That said, let us now look at some measures introduced to tackle the black money menace in real estate.[75] The Benami Transactions Amendment Act 2016[76] was thought of as one key deterrent to investing black money in real estate. A *benami*[77] transaction is defined as a transaction wherein a property is held by or transferred in the name of a person but has been provided or paid for by another person. The definition also includes property transactions where i) a transaction has been made under a fictitious name; ii) the owner is not aware or denies knowledge of the ownership of the

---

L/Opinion-divided-over-impact-of-demonetisation-on-real-estate.html

[75] In my opinion, many of these measures have not had great success. This is based on my travels and experience across India both before and after November, 2016. That is why I have suggested radical reforms proposed in this book including abolition of income tax, introduction of BTT, rationalization of GST, revision of property guideline values in line with market values and reduction of stamp duty and registration fees on real estate transactions as discussed later in this chapter and throughout this book.

[76] See 'The Benami Transactions (Prohibition) Amendment Act, 2016, No. 43 Of 2016, August 10, 2016, *Ministry of Law and Justice*, The Gazette of India',
http://www.prsindia.org/uploads/media/Benami/Benami%20Transactions%20Act,%202016.pdf

[77] Benami is a Persian language word that means "without name" or "no name". In this Act, the word is used to define a transaction in which the real beneficiary is not the one in whose name the property is purchased. As a result, the person in whose name the property is purchased is just a mask for the real beneficiary.

property; iii) the person providing the property is not traceable.

Benami transactions originally came into being post the Central Government's enactment of the Urban Land (Ceiling and Regulation) Act in1976 and the Agricultural Land Ceiling Acts enacted by the various state governments with a view to ensuring equitable distribution of land amongst the people. In order to protect their existing land holdings, people transferred sections of their property to the names of their relatives and trusted confidantes to be held in trust until such time as they needed to liquidate it. Likewise, those making fresh acquisitions, particularly using black money, also preferred to invest in the names of family members and friends with a view to escape the scrutiny of the tax authorities as well as the revenue officials. The Urban Land Ceiling Act was repealed in 1999 while the Agricultural Land Reform legislations remain in operation in several Indian states.

The Benami Transactions Amendment Act 2016, basically an amendment to the Benami Transactions (Prohibition) Act of 1988, proposed the creation of an authority for the acquisition of property acquired through *benami*[78] means, and also laid down punitive measures including possible imprisonment or penalties or both. However, in keeping with the

---

[78] Benami is a **Persian language** word that means "without name" or "no name". In this Act, the word is used to define a transaction in which the real beneficiary is not the one in whose name the property is purchased. As a result, the person in whose name the property is purchased is just a mask for the real beneficiary.

thought of influencing and enabling compliance rather than enforcing it, the Income Declaration Scheme (IDS), 2016 was implemented for the voluntary declaration of undisclosed income, including disclosure of non-cash assets like moveable or immoveable assets, gold and jewellery. The undisclosed income was to be taxed at a flat rate of 45 percent.[79] As per Circular No. 17 of 2016 dated 20th May, 2016 and Circular No. 24 of 2016 dated 27th June, 2016, such assets were accorded immunity[80] under the Income-tax Act, 1961, the Wealth-tax Act, 1957 and the Benami Transactions (Prohibition) Act, 1988 providing certain conditions were met.

The same provisions are applicable to the disclosure of gold and jewellery also. By laying down that with non-disclosure, an assessee runs the risk of forfeiture, the punitive aspect has also been addressed. Backed up by income tax scrutiny and investigations, these were expected to serve as sufficient motivation to declare all undisclosed income in whatever form, and serve as a fair deterrent for the future. The Income Tax department notified[81] that the Benami

---

[79] See 'The Income Declaration Scheme 2016 to open from 1st June 2016', May 14, 2016, *Press Information Bureau*, Government of India, Ministry of Finance,
http://pib.nic.in/newsite/PrintRelease.aspx?relid=145360

[80] See 'Clarifications on the Income Declaration Scheme, 2016', June 30, 2016, Circular No. 25 of 2016, Government of India, Ministry of Finance, Department of Revenue Central Board of Direct Taxes,
http://www.incometaxindia.gov.in/communications/circular/circular252016.pdf

[81] See 'Benami Transactions (Prohibition) Amendment Act, 2016 To Come In To Effect From Tomorrow [Read Bill]', October 31, 2016, *LiveLaw.in*, Vidushi Sahani, http://www.livelaw.in/benami-

Transactions (Prohibition) Amendment Act, 2016 (BTP Amendment Act), came into force from November 1, 2016.

In addition, from the beginning of 2016, the Government has been insisting on PAN[82] numbers for gold and jewellery transactions upwards of Rs 2 lakh, term deposits upwards of Rs 5 lakh, shares and stocks valued at upward of Rs 1 lakh and real estate valued at over Rs 10 lakh. This is to facilitate the easy retrieval of information and to facilitate matching of information relating to investment, raising of loans and other business activities of taxpayers collected through various sources, both internal as well as external. This step again was expected to help in detecting and combating tax evasion and also, widening of the tax base.[83]

---

transactions-prohibition-amendment-act-2016-come-effect-tomorrow-read-bill/

[82] See 'PAN/TAN',
http://www.incometaxindia.gov.in/Pages/pan.aspx Permanent Account Number (PAN) is a ten-digit alphanumeric number, issued in the form of a laminated card, by the Income Tax Department, to any "person" who applies for it or to whom the department allots the number without an application. PAN enables the department to link all transactions of the "person" with the department. These transactions include tax payments, TDS/TCS credits, returns of income/wealth/gift/FBT, specified transactions, correspondence, and so on. PAN, thus, acts as an identifier for the "person" with the tax department.

[83] In my opinion, many of these measures have not had great success. This is based on my travels and experience across India both before and after November, 2016. That is why I have suggested radical reforms proposed in this book including abolition of income tax, introduction of BTT, rationalization of GST, revision of property guideline values in line with market values and reduction of stamp duty and registration fees on real estate transactions as discussed later in this chapter and throughout this book.

Coming back to the critical role of the real estate sector in contributing to GDP growth, and also its role as the second largest employment generator, the sector's well-being is crucial to the health of the larger economy—there are no two ways about this fact.

In fact, the importance of the real estate sector for growth of the Indian economy can be gauged from the fact that in 2013, the then Chairman of the Confederation of Real Estate Developers Associations of India, Pradeep Jain, called for reforms[84] to the sector, considering how critical the sector was for the Government to achieve growth targets of even 7-8 percent per annum.

The sector is said to impact more than 250 manufacturing and services industries including steel and cement. Apart from industry level concessions, tax rebates and project finance, certain other concessions need to be extended to ensure the health of the sector in the interest of the investors as well as the economy.

The above apart, what is critical is an immediate rationalization of guideline values[85] of properties in the revenue department records, making them more in tune with the actual rates that prevail in the

---

[84] See 'Reforms in real estate key to GDP growth: Credai', January 6, 2013, *The Hindu Business Line*,
http://www.thehindubusinessline.com/news/real-estate/reforms-in-real-estate-key-to-gdp-growth-credai/article4279859.ece

[85] This needs to be undertaken by the respective state governments.

markets. Even where parties to a transaction are willing to record the entire sale value,[86] they are often dissuaded by the revenue officials themselves on the grounds that it would set a precedent and prove a deterrent to other parties wanting to avail themselves of the benefits of low property guideline values.

A rationalization of the property guideline values with the prevailing market rates would force the transacting parties to register the sale at actual cost rather than a fraction of it, thereby eliminating the black money component in the transaction. That is the key point that needs to be noted here. And with rationalization, it would become next to impossible for the sector to absorb black money the way it is doing currently.

A rule of thumb can be applied for correcting the property guideline value—increase the guideline value by 5 to 6 times for rural areas, 3 to 4 times for peri-urban areas and 2 to 3 times for urban areas. As someone with grassroots level experience of having worked across 640 districts across the country, this is a simple heuristic I suggest to arrive at initial estimates for revising the guideline value. These can subsequently be adjusted as per actual demand and prevailing market rates, on a regular basis.

Stamp duties and registration charges are the other important components in any real estate transaction

---

[86] In many cases, the seller is ready to accept all money via the bank but the buyers are reluctant because they cannot show a proper source for the monies provided. This then forces legitimate tax abiding sellers also to accept black (unaccounted) money.

and they too need to be rationalized[87] across India to further eliminate the black money component. Both these revenue receipts accrue to the individual states, and the Central government has no jurisdiction over them. Going by 2014–15 budget estimates, the total revenue accruing to the states from stamp duty and registration charges stood at Rs 98,040 crore,[88] at a little under 8 percent of the total state revenues from all sources. They rank third among all direct state revenues, after state sales tax (43 percent) and state excise duties (8 percent).

Since stamp duty and registration fees are calculated as a percentage of the total value of the transaction, rationalizing guideline values will result in a huge increase in the transaction costs related to any property purchase. Since it is incumbent on the buyer to pay stamp duty and registration fees, he would prefer to undervalue the consideration quoted in the deed of sale to save on the costs of stamp duty and registration charges. The current stamp duty rates range[89] from as low as 4 percent to as high as 10 percent.

---

[87] See 'Slash stamp duty to clean up real estate sector: Assocham', November 14, 2016, *The Economic Times,* PTI, http://economictimes.indiatimes.com/wealth/real-estate/slash-stamp-duty-to-clean-up-real-estate-sector-assocham/articleshow/55413511.cms?from=mdr

[88] See 'Indian Public Finance Statistics 2014-2015', July, 2015 *Ministry of Finance, Department of Economic Affairs and Economic Division,* Government of India, http://finmin.nic.in/reports/IPFStat201415.pdf

[89] See appendix 1d for a listing of stamp duty rates across states in India.

The National Housing Bank, which is a subsidiary of the RBI, must work along with the registration department in different states to rationalize and reduce stamp duties. At no point or in no state should stamp duty and registration fees be in excess of 1 percent of the guideline value, in line with the best practices the world over. No loss to the exchequer is expected from this downward revision of stamp duties and registration fees to 1 percent as property guideline values would have been commensurately increased to reflect true market values. Also, the BTT component, as proposed in this book, is Rs 0.75 per Rs 100. This BTT yields a total of Rs 21.65 lakh crore using FY 2018-19 RBI payment system data, which is far in excess of the direct and indirect tax collection (in FY 2018-19) of Rs 11.37 lakh crore and Rs 9.39 lakh crore respectively. This coupled with a fact that a flat GST of 5 percent is also being levied should provide enough surplus and cushion to offset and absorb any potential reduction in stamp duty and registration fees collection that may arise due to reduction of stamp duties and registration fees.

In the current situation of unrealistic guideline values and exorbitant stamp duty charges, people will resort to undervaluing the properties to avoid paying taxes, and this will only result in a loss to the exchequer. This will also have a cascading effect[90] since the

---

[90] See 'Stamp Duties in Indian States: A Case for Reform', September 2004, *World Bank Policy Research Working Paper 3413*, James Alm, Patricia Annez, and Arbind Modi,
http://documents.worldbank.org/curated/en/775111468750283848/pdf/WPS3413.pdf

transaction value will have a direct bearing on other taxes like property tax, wealth tax and gift tax.

A recursive cycle will be set off where, in order to avoid revealing the existence of this black money, the individual or the company must utilize it in ways that maintain secrecy. The monies derived from undervaluation/evasion cannot be brought into the books of accounts and hence cannot be used for legitimate or official transactions. Such monies accumulated through such unaccounted means produce a cascading effect through the entire production process, as activities must continue to remain hidden. Put differently, the underreporting incentive in property sale and stamp duties feeds the "black economy" by driving more such unaccounted money and resources into the sector, which then multiplies even further as it is used to fuel a variety of transactions in the black or the parallel economy.

For example, the most frequent recipients of the unaccounted funds would be property builders who, in turn, will continue to have incentives to circulate this unaccounted cash in the parallel (black) economy. And the further this money circulates, it fuels a whole range of other transactions that fall out of the ambit of the tax system. For example, cash payments to raw materials suppliers result in loss of sales tax and excise duties. Likewise, property builders who receive the payments as cash avoid showing these receipts as income and hence, evade income tax. Taken together, all these recipients of the unaccounted black (cash) money start the cycle of buying goods and services in the black economy, all of which continue to escape the tax net with a huge cascading effect. The net result is that not only are stamp duty and registration fees avoided but a whole range of taxes are lost both by the central and state governments. Also, black attracts more black in the sense that the scope for undervalued transactions and tax evasion thereon attract more and more people who are looking for ways to 'unofficially' invest their unaccounted for wealth.

Effectively, if rationalization of guideline values and stamp duty charges happens, it directly eliminates the scope for a black money component in real estate transactions, since there is no scope to conceal or evade.

The Real Estate (Regulation and Development) Bill,[91] 2016, which became an act on May 1, has kick-started the process of putting in place an institutional infrastructure to protect the interests of home buyers in India. From an honest, tax-paying buyer's perspective, this is a welcome step. If the revision of guideline values is also effected across various states of India, it would effectively mean that he would be able to reflect the entire value of his acquisition in his book of assets and also raise loans from the formal financial institutions to finance his transaction.

---

[91] See 'Real Estate Bill is an act now, may protect home buyers', May 2, 2016, *The Economic Times,* Ravi Teja Sharma, http://economictimes.indiatimes.com/wealth/real-estate/real-estate-bill-is-an-act-now-may-protect-home-buyers/articleshow/52069308.cms

Corruption at the level of the planning bodies[92] also needs addressing, since builders/developers end up passing on the bribes paid to hasten the process of acquiring permits/licenses/permissions to the buyers in the form of the black money component of the sale price.

Yet another aspect that needs consideration is the percentage of sale proceeds that a seller would need to pay into the exchequer in the form of capital gains tax if it is a non-agricultural asset, or as a higher income tax in certain other scenarios like short term capital gains. There are exemptions to long term capital gains if the sale proceeds are reinvested within a stipulated time frame. Overall, as recommended in the earlier chapter, the abolition of capital gains tax too would help in keeping the real estate sector black money free. Indeed, as already suggested, with the abolition of income tax, the associated capital gains tax will also have to go.

Tax reforms on all these fronts might also yield unexpected benefits in the form of retaining some portion of domestic capital that is otherwise invested in real estate outside India. India[93] ranks eighth from the top in a list of countries by the amount of land acquired abroad. Indian companies have been among the biggest investors in land in countries like

---

[92] This would include state, regional and local planning bodies that provide permissions for plot development and building construction.
[93] See 'Indian direct investment', June 29, 2015, *The Indian Express*, Christophe Jaffrelot,
http://indianexpress.com/article/opinion/columns/indian-direct-investment/

Cambodia, Indonesia, Madagascar, Kenya and Ethiopia. The Indian government is itself a major investor in land abroad, especially in East Africa. Indians are also the largest non-Arab investors in Dubai. However, it is the West that holds the most attraction for Indian companies investing in property abroad. For example, the Lodha Group is said to have planned an investment over £5 billion in the last few and coming years in developing property in London, which will be among the largest known foreign direct investment (FDI) in real estate that the U.K. will have ever received. In FY 2013-14, the Indians were ranked fourth, only behind the Canadians, Chinese and Mexicans, in investing in properties in U.S. cities.

While on the one hand, India continues to try to attract FDI[94] in real estate, here we have a reverse flow happening. Though there may be a certain element of prestige associated with the acquisition of real estate in prime global spots, the 'messy' state of affairs in Indian real estate is surely a reason too. The lack of transparency in deals, the high levels of unaccounted money and the degree of corruption encountered in the process of acquiring approvals and permits for real estate projects, from the revenue and the planning authorities, all possibly serve as

---

[94] See 'Indian Government Announces FDI in Real Estate to Benefit the Real Estate Growth', November 17, 2015, *Business Wire*, The Hindu Business Line,
http://www.thehindubusinessline.com/news/real-estate/indian-government-announces-fdi-in-real-estate-to-benefit-the-real-estate-growth/article7886880.ece

deterrents in attracting FDI as also helping to retain domestic capital within the country.

In the wake of demonetization, it was thought that it would be extremely difficult to structure real estate deals with a black money component. It was considered that the reserves lost then might take time to build up all over again, except for what might have already been routed out of the country to be brought back through other means.

However, if we look at what is happening in real estate in India in 2019, the same trend of registering at low guideline values has continued and a significant proportion of the land registration is taking place with a huge black money component[95].

State governments have played a role in perhaps unknowingly encouraging this by enhancing the stamp duties and reducing the guideline values further when they should have implemented the reverse instead (lower stamp duties and higher guidelines values).

The case of Tamil Nadu, where stamp duty and registration fees have been increased from 8 percent (7 percent + 1 percent) to 11 percent (7 percent + 4 percent) coupled with a reduction in guideline values by almost 1/3rd the previous value[96] is a great

---

[95] This is based on my travels and experience across India both before and after November, 2016.
[96] See 'Tamil Nadu has second highest property registration cost among states', July 13, 2019, Jayaraj Sivan, The Times of India,

example of how and why black money in real estate refuses to go away.

The above has to change, and in the realty sector, stamp duty and registration fees for property and other documents must be rationalized as outlined below:

a) At no time, should stamp duty and registration fees[97] exceed 1 percent of total property guideline value (GV) which must also be increased as per the following rules of thumb:
   - ☞ increase existing GV by 5 to 6 times in rural areas;
   - ☞ increase existing GV by 3 to 4 times in peri urban areas; and

---

https://timesofindia.indiatimes.com/city/chennai/tn-has-2nd-highest-property-regn-cost-among-states/articleshow/70199925.cms
See 'Guideline value cut by 33% in T.N.', June 8, 2017, Dennis S. Jesudasan, https://www.thehindu.com/news/national/tamil-nadu/tn-government-slashes-guideline-value-by-33/article18853030.ece
See 'Circular to Public', Registration Department, Government of Tamil Nadu, http://www.tnreginet.net/circular/public_Circulars/Circular_Guideline_Reduction_RF_Revision.pdf

[97] No loss to the exchequer is expected from this downward revision of stamp duties and registration fees to 1 percent as property guideline values would have been commensurately increased to reflect true market values. Also, the BTT component, as proposed in this book, is Rs 0.75 per Rs 100. This BTT yields a total of Rs 21.65 lakh crore using FY 2018-19 RBI payment system data, which is far in excess of the direct and indirect tax collection (in FY 2018-19) of Rs 11.37 lakh crore and Rs 9.39 lakh crore respectively. This coupled with a fact that a flat GST of 5 percent is also being levied should provide enough surplus and cushion to offset and absorb any potential reduction in stamp duty and registration fees collection that may arise due to reduction of stamp duties and registration fees.

☞ increase existing GV by 2 to 3 times in urban areas;

b) The assistance of the National Housing Bank, a subsidiary of RBI can be taken in this regard and a national level database created with regard to land guideline values across the various states of India. This has to be updated on a regular, at least annual basis so that guideline values are in line with market values.

Coupled with the earlier measures for direct taxes especially, the above will help eliminate the single largest source of black money in India.

Overall, the importance of the real estate sector in kick-starting the Indian economy cannot be stressed upon enough. There are allied industries like construction, cement, steel and others that feed into the real estate sector. Increased activity in all of these industries would contribute to the sector's growth and thereby enhance its contribution to overall employment and income generation.

If the suggested reforms in this chapter are carried out in the interim and corruption eliminated from the process of acquiring licenses and approval of real estate project permits, and if compliance with safety standards and other requisites are ensured, the realty sector might be able to survive the drying up of the lubricant that kept it well-oiled and find ways to reinvent itself without losing its inherent strengths.

Without a doubt, a vibrant real estate sector should help to (re)create millions of jobs and thereby bolster the growth of the Indian economy. If the Indian economy is to grow at rates greater than 15 percent, then, undoubtedly, reforms in the real estate sector would have to play a huge role in the economic reforms process.

Chapter 3

Restructure the Lokpal and Lokayuktas

If there is even a single point of convergence in the various corruption debates, including the 2016 demonetization debate, it is the fact that black money is the fuel that keeps the engine of corruption humming. If tax evasion is the seed that brings forth the black money tree, then corruption is the fruit that it bears. The product of an illegal action can neither be acknowledged in the open nor recognized as a component of a lawful transaction. So it needs to be recognized that black money brings forth more corruption and serves to generate more of its kind and the cycle goes on.

What did demonetization truly achieve in the context of corruption? For one, it extinguished the value of the black money hoarded in the open market. While the declaration on the night of November 8, 2016 achieved that, it did give an opportunity for the black money to be brought into the formal financial system at a fraction of its value, with the major portion being absorbed by the state in the form of taxes and penalties. This way, a trail would be established and the tax authorities would keep a closer watch over the sources of the surrendered black money.

However, there is a lot of debate on how successful the demonetization exercise was in mopping up the currency in circulation in the form of the SBNs, and the black money component in the same. Even back then, what is distressing is that the exercise does not appear to have completely succeeded in putting the fear of the law in the hearts of all the people.

There were reports of the corrupt resorting to various techniques including the use of money mules to get their stash of black money white-washed and several bank officials[98] were reportedly charged with abetting hoarders in having their black money reserves converted to newly minted currency. Hardly a week after the demonetization, two officials[99] of the Kandla port in Gujarat were found to have

---

[98] See 'Demonetisation: 27 senior bank officials suspended to check corrupt practices', December 2, 2016, *The Times of India*, PTI, http://timesofindia.indiatimes.com/india/Demonetisation-27-senior-bank-officials-suspended-to-check-corrupt-practices/articleshow/55753967.cms

[99] See 'Demonetisation: Three held for accepting bribe in new currency', November 17, 2016, *The Indian Express*, PTI, http://indianexpress.com/article/india/india-news-india/demonetisation-three-held-for-accepting-bribe-in-new-currency-4380715/

accepted bribes, in newly minted Rs 2,000 notes. This was not an isolated report, though. There were too many of them over the weeks (following demonetization) to dismiss them as such. And nearly three years after demonetization, I am not sure that the level of black money in circulation has decreased in any significant manner. The earlier chapter on real estate stands testimony to this.

Such brazenness, in the face of what can possibly be termed one of the country's biggest and boldest measures against black money, only goes to prove the point that demonetization can only be the first step, and certainly not the only one, to win the war against black money or corruption. More importantly, this first step has not been a sufficient deterrent for the corrupt that occupy the echelons of power.

So, if we're really serious about eradicating black money, we need to first find ways to uproot the corruption that is at its base. Corruption is, after all, the all-important source of black money, and creates a chain of events and practices that become self-sustaining and ultimately consume the system.

Before we seek ways to put an end to 'corruption', it would be useful to define the term. In my opinion, corruption is a very complex phenomenon, with its roots digging deep into the functioning of political, bureaucratic, commercial and non-governmental institutions and involving a variety of stakeholders in both the public and private sectors.

In definitional terms, corruption is any action (or set

of actions) where institutions/people abuse their (public/private) office for private gain. It requires two or more parties acting in concert—parties who are misusing the office and parties who benefit from such misuse. Such an abuse of office for private gain happens when the individuals/institutions concerned accept, solicit, and/or extort a bribe. It is also misuse of power when intermediaries/agents actively offer bribes to circumvent policies and processes for competitive advantage and profit. An act can also be construed as corruption even if no bribery occurs— for example, through patronage and nepotism based on family/other relationships,[100] the theft of state/private institutional assets by people in positions of power,[101] and/or the diversion of state/institutional revenues to private parties.

Corruption can further be categorised as either spectacular corruption (like in the case of various scams—2G Spectrum[102] or Commonwealth Games[103] or Bellary Mines[104] or Coal Block

---

[100] See appendix 5 for examples of the 'revolving door phenomenon' that caused huge conflicts of interest in the United States.

[101] See appendix 6 for examples of 'conflicts of interests' in the financial sector in the United States.

[102] See 'What is the 2G spectrum scam?', October 19, 2012, *India Today*, http://indiatoday.intoday.in/story/what-is-the-2g-scam-all-about/1/188832.html

[103] See 'Major scam hits Commonwealth Games', July 31, 2010, The Hindu, PTI, http://www.thehindu.com/news/national/Major-scam-hits-Commonwealth-Games/article16215706.ece

[104] See 'Karnataka lost Rs 1 lakh cr from 2006-2010', June 17, 2013, The Hindu, Sudipto Mondal, http://www.thehindu.com/news/national/karnataka/karnataka-lost-rs-1-lakh-cr-from-20062010/article4820758.ece

Allocation[105] or Adarsh Housing Society[106] or the Harshad Mehta Scam)[107] or the PNB/IL&FS[108] scams[109] or regular corruption (bribes to get things done on a day-to-day basis).

---

[105] See 'What's the coal scam about?', March 12, 2015, The Hindu, Special Correspondent,
http://www.thehindu.com/news/national/whats-the-coal-scam-about/article6983434.ece

[106] See 'Adarsh scam: The story of a posh high-rise with not-so-posh occupants', April 29, 2016, The Hindu, Deepalakshmi K,
http://www.thehindu.com/news/national/Adarsh-scam-The-story-of-a-posh-high-rise-with-not-so-posh-occupants/article14264528.ece

[107] See 'Economic Milestone: Stock Market Scam (1992)', August 20, 2014, *Forbes India Magazine,* Pravin Palande,
http://www.forbesindia.com/article/independence-day-special/economic-milestone-stock-market-scam-(1992)/38457/1

[108] PNB= Punjab National Bank and Infrastructure Leasing & Financial Services Limited (IL&FS)

[109] In 2018, one of India's biggest bank frauds occurred, and it was allegedly carried out by Nirav Modi, Mehul Choksi and associates at PNB—it has been reported that Nirav Modi and his uncle Mehul Choksi, in connivance with certain bank officials, allegedly cheated PNB of about Rs 14,000 crore (which is close to U.S. $2 billion) through issuance of fraudulent letters of undertaking (LoUs). Likewise, the IL&FS scam is a noteworthy one in the Indian financial and infrastructure sector. Specifically, between July 2018 and September 2018, two subsidiaries of the IL&FS Group reportedly experienced trouble in paying back loans and inter-corporate deposits to banks/lenders. In July 2018, the road arm of IL&FS is said to have faced similar difficulty in making repayments due on its bonds. Further, in early September 2018, one of the subsidiaries of IL&FS Group defaulted in repaying a short-term loan of Rs 1,000 crore to Small Industries Development Bank of India (SIDBI). Simultaneously, it was also alleged that the affairs of IL&FS were being conducted in a manner prejudicial to the public interest. For example, Ravi Parthasarathy and other senior management personnel (i.e., Ravi Parthasarathy, Hari Sankaran and Arun K Saha) were said to be running IL&FS as their personal fiefdoms and taking irrational compensation, despite IL&FS's huge debt burden of ~ Rs 1064 billion and dramatic losses of ~ Rs 18.87 billion in 2017-18.—See 'Never Waste A Crisis', November 2018, Ramesh S Arunachalam for a complete background into the IL&FS scam..

Spectacular corruption is often remembered while the institutionalized day to day corruption in the form of bribery, including corporate bribery, is so entrenched in our system that it is almost accepted as a way of life. However, bribery in general and corporate bribery, in particular, is bad for the environment, especially in a free market economy that India aspires to become—where fair competition should determine who wins at the market place, be it for the supply of products or services rendered. That products and services should compete on the basis of price, quality, service, and other factors is undisputed. Corporate bribery destroys this basic tenet and corporations bribing officials to assist in gaining business is bad practice.

Of course, one must also not forget fraud and associated evils that can and do take place in the private/public sector, often with disastrous and costly results. Many of these result in the accumulation of illegal wealth and black money. Weakly regulated and fraudulent financial systems can undermine people's savings, increase transaction costs, enhance indebtedness and impose high economic costs when they collapse. The 2010 Andhra Pradesh microfinance crisis[110] is a case in point as also the sub-prime crisis[111] in the United States and elsewhere.

---

[110] See appendix 7 for what happened in the Indian microfinance sector in 2010—called as the 2010 Andhra Pradesh microfinance crisis.
[111] See appendix 6 for what happened in the United States 'sub-prime' mortgages market.

The Satyam Computers fiasco is yet another example worth recalling here. This suggests that corporate crime,[112] which typically takes any of the following forms, is yet another form of corruption that also leads to accumulation of black money. The examples include: a) misrepresentation in financial statements of corporations; b) manipulation in the stock market; c) securities fraud; d) conflicts of interests; e) commercial bribery including that of public officials directly or indirectly; f) embezzlement and misappropriation of funds; g) misapplication of funds in receiverships and bankruptcies; and h) taxation related issues including use of tax havens and so on.

The above, in many ways, suggest the broad context of corruption in India. The key question here is how can this multifaceted phenomenon of corruption be fought so as to eliminate black money emanating from all of these?

One way would be to use the Lokpal[113] and its state counterparts (Lokayuktas) as an institutional response to fight corruption and thereby possibly curb black money. Indeed, the Indian Parliament

---

[112] See 'The Scam: from Harshad Mehta to Ketan Parekh Also includes JPC FIASCO & Global Trust Bank Scam', *Kensource Information Services Private Limited*, Debshish Basu and Sucheta Dalal, https://www.amazon.in/SCAM-Harshad-Parekh-FIASCO-Global-ebook/dp/B00M8XSXWY, which offers interesting insights regarding securities fraud and related matters.
[113] See 'Why Lokpal eludes India 30 months after Parliament passed a historic law', May 30, 2016, *The Times of India*, Darpan Singh in Mirror Image, http://blogs.timesofindia.indiatimes.com/darpan-singh-blog/why-lokpal-eludes-india-30-months-after-parliament-passed-a-historic-law/

passed the Lokpal and Lokayuktas Act, 2013[114] facilitating the establishment of a Lokpal (Ombudsman) with the specific objective of fighting corruption in public offices and ensuring accountability of all public officials, including the Prime Minister (PM), but with some special safeguards.

As per this law, the Lokpal is to consist of a chairperson and a maximum of eight members with 50 percent of them as judicial members and the remaining 50 percent comprising scheduled castes (SC), scheduled tribes (ST), other backward classes (OBCs), minorities and women. The chairperson and members of Lokpal are to be selected by a committee consisting of the Prime Minister (PM), the Speaker of the Lok Sabha, the Leader of Opposition in the Lok Sabha and the Chief Justice of India (CJI) or a sitting Supreme Court judge nominated by CJI. An eminent jurist is to be nominated as a fifth member by the President of India on the basis of recommendations of the first four members of the selection committee "through consensus".

Lokpal's jurisdiction is to cover all types and categories of public servants. In addition, all entities (including NGOs) who receive foreign donations—as per the Foreign Contribution Regulation Act (FCRA)—in excess of Rs 10 lakh per year are to

---

[114] See 'The Lokpal And Lokayuktas Act 2013', January 1, 2014, *Ministry of Law and Justice*, The Gazette Of India Extraordinary Part II, http://www.indiacode.nic.in/acts2014/1%20of%202014.pdf and 'The Lokpal and Lokayuktas Act, 2013', *Wikipedia*, https://en.wikipedia.org/wiki/Lokpal_and_Lokayuktas_Act,_2013

come under the purview of the Lokpal. Furthermore, states are to set up their respective Lokayuktas through an appropriate state law within 365 days.

The fact of the matter though is that India got a Lokpal only in March 2019, over five years after the bill was passed in Parliament. Part of the reason for this is the non-availability of the Leader of the Opposition in the Lok Sabha for the search committee.

It is my opinion that the central government must bring an amendment to the Lokpal and Lokayuktas Act, 2013 that will permit the Leader of the Opposition (in the Rajya Sabha) to be a part of the search committee whenever there is no recognized Leader of Opposition in the Lok Sabha.

That said, Lokayuktas have been established in the following states: Andhra Pradesh,[115] Assam,[116] Bihar,[117] Chhattisgarh,[118] Delhi,[119] Gujarat,[120]

---

[115] See 'The Andhra Pradesh Lokayukta and Upa Lokayukta (Amendment) Act, 1987', *Laws of India*, http://www.lawsofindia.org/statelaw/1711/TheAndhraPradeshLokayuktaandUpaLokayuktaAmendmentAct1987.html

[116] See 'The Assam Lokayukta and Upa-Lokayuktas Act, 1985', *Laws of India*, http://www.lawsofindia.org/statelaw/6126/TheAssamLokayuktaandUpaLokayuktasAct1985.html

[117] See 'The Bihar Lokayukta Act, 1973', http://lokayukta.bih.nic.in/Act.htm

[118] See 'The Chhattisgarh Lok Aayog Act, 2002', *Laws of India*, http://www.lawsofindia.org/statelaw/2851/TheChhattisgarhLokAayogAct2002.html

[119] See 'The Delhi Lokayukta and Upalokayukta Act, 1995', *Laws of India*,

Haryana,[121] Himachal Pradesh,[122] Uttar Pradesh,[123] Madhya Pradesh,[124] West Bengal,[125] Tamil Nadu,[126] Kerala,[127] Karnataka,[128] Rajasthan,[129] Jharkhand,[130] Punjab,[131] Sikkim,[132] Tripura,[133] Meghalaya,[134]

---

http://www.lawsofindia.org/statelaw/2780/TheDelhiLokayuktaandUpalokayuktaAct1995.html

[120] See 'The Gujarat Lokayukta Act, 1986', *Laws of India*, http://www.lawsofindia.org/statelaw/2196/TheGujaratLokayuktaAct1986.html

[121] See 'The Haryana Lokayukta Act, 2002', *Laws of India*, http://www.lawsofindia.org/statelaw/1305/TheHaryanaLokayuktaAct2002.html

[122] See 'The Himachal Pradesh Lokayukta Act, 1983', *Laws of India*, http://www.lawsofindia.org/statelaw/3085/TheHimachalPradeshLokayuktaAct1983.html

[123] See 'The Uttar Pradesh Lokayukta and Up-Lokayuktas (Amendment) Act, 1981', *Laws of India*, http://www.lawsofindia.org/pdf/uttar_pradesh/1981/1981UP7.pdf

[124] See 'The Madhya Pradesh Lokayukt and Up-Lokayukt Act, 1981', http://www.mplokayukt.nic.in/Adhiniyam1981.pdf

[125] See 'The West Bengal Lokayukta Act, 2003', http://wbpar.gov.in/writereaddata/11076.pdf

[126] See 'The Tamil Nadu Lokayukta Act, 2018', http://www.stationeryprinting.tn.gov.in/extraordinary/2018/380_Ex_III_1a.pdf

[127] See 'The Kerala Lok Ayukta Act, 1999', https://www.lokayuktakerala.gov.in/staticinfo/act1999.php

[128] See 'The Karnataka Lokayukta Act, 1984', *Laws of India*, http://www.lawsofindia.org/statelaw/74315/TheKarnatakaLokayuktaAct1984.html

[129] See 'The Rajasthan Lokayukta and Up-Lokayuktas Act, 1973', *Laws of India*, http://www.lawsofindia.org/statelaw/7624/TheRajasthanLokayuktaandUpLokayuktasAct1973.html

[130] See 'The Jharkhand Lokayukta Act, 2001', http://lokayuktajharkhand.nic.in/Act.html

[131] See 'Punjab Lokpal Act 1996', http://lokpal.punjab.gov.in/index.php/acts-rules

[132] See 'The Sikkim Lokayukta Act, 2012', *Laws of India*, http://www.lawsofindia.org/pdf/sikkim/2012/2012Sikkim21.pdf

Mizoram,[135] Manipur[136] and Odisha.[137] The central government must engage in dialogue with the other state governments and ensure that they too have functioning Lokayuktas in their respective states, at least within a time period of one year.

Here, it must be mentioned that the present government has introduced and passed 'the Lokpal and Lokayuktas (Amendment[138]) Bill, 2016' in the Lok Sabha[139] to amend the Lokpal and Lokayuktas Act, 2013 in relation to the declaration of assets and liabilities by public servants[140]. The provisions of the Bill are to apply retrospectively, from the date of the coming into force of the 2013 Act.

While the Lokpal bill has been passed by Parliament, a number of other bills, which will provide a sound

---

[133] See 'The Tripura Lokayukta Act, 2008', *Laws of India*, http://www.lawsofindia.org/statelaw/74298/TheTripuraLokayuktaAct2008.html

[134] See 'The Meghalaya Lokayukta Act, 2014', http://www.lawsofindia.org/pdf/meghalaya/2014/2014Meghalaya4.pdf

[135] See 'The Mizoram Lokayukta (Amendment) Act, 2016', https://indiacode.nic.in/bitstream/123456789/8983/1/ex-398.pdf

[136] See 'The Manipur Lokayukta Act, 2014', https://manipur.gov.in/wp-content/uploads/2018/10/manipurlokayuktarules.pdf

[137] See 'The Lokpal and Lokayuktas Act, 1995', *Laws of India*, http://www.lawsofindia.org/statelaw/2626/TheLokpalandLokayuktasAct1995.html

[138] See 'The Lokpal and Lokayuktas (Amendment) Bill, 2016', *PRS India*, http://www.prsindia.org/billtrack/the-lokpal-and-lokayuktas-bill-2016-4354/

[139] On July 27, 2016.

[140] In my opinion, the amendment is likely to weaken the fight against corruption as it is likely to enhance the play of conflict of interest in the public sector.

basis for tackling corruption, are still pending[141] in Parliament. These include bills related to citizen charter,[142] electronic public service delivery,[143] and public procurement.[144] The judicial accountability bill[145], the *Benami* transactions bill[146] and Whistleblower protection bill[147] have, however, been passed. Together, all of these bills, when they become fully operational, should facilitate the Lokpal to deal with the issue of corruption in a more comprehensive manner.

---

[141] This is true as at the time of writing this book and to the best of my knowledge as well.

[142] See 'The Right of Citizens for Time Bound Delivery of Goods and Services and Redressal of their Grievances Bill, 2011 (Citizens Charter)', *PRS India,* http://www.prsindia.org/billtrack/the-right-of-citizens-for-time-bound-delivery-of-goods-and-services-and-redressal-of-their-grievances-bill-2011-2125/, **Current Status: Lapsed**

[143] See 'The Electronic Delivery of Services Bill, 2011', *PRS India, http://www.prsindia.org/billtrack/the-electronic-delivery-of-services-bill-2011-2148/,* **Current Status: Lapsed**

[144] See 'The Public Procurement Bill, 2012', *PRS India,* http://www.prsindia.org/billtrack/the-public-procurement-bill-2012-2310/, **Current Status: Lapsed**

[145] See 'The Judicial Standards and Accountability Bill, 2010', *PRS India,* http://www.prsindia.org/billtrack/the-judicial-standards-and-accountability-bill-2010-1399/, **Current Status: Passed by Lok Sabha, March 29, 2012.**

[146] See 'The Benami Transactions (Prohibition) (Amendment) Bill, 2015', *PRS India,* http://www.prsindia.org/billtrack/the-benami-transactions-prohibition-amendment-bill-2015-3789/, **Current Status: Passed by Lok Sabha (July 27, 2016) and Rajya Sabha (August 2, 2016)**

[147] See 'The Whistle Blowers Protection (Amendment) Bill, 2015', *PRS India,* http://www.prsindia.org/billtrack/the-whistle-blowers-protection-amendment-bill-2015-3784/, **Current Status: Passed by Lok Sabha (May 13, 2015)**

While enacting a law is the first step towards curbing corruption, the effectiveness of the law would depend on how well it is implemented on the ground. This leads one to ask, how can the Lokpal be made effective to help fight this menace? What are the implications for the design and implementation of the Lokpal as an institutionalized response to fight corruption?

First, let us clearly recognize the fact that while the RTI (Right to Information) Act was perhaps the first baby step in this process, an effective Lokpal is a big and crucial step.

Second, to be effective, the Lokpal must be appropriately designed. Specifically, the scope of the Lokpal must clearly be thought out in terms of who the Act will cover and for what kinds of corruption. Care must be devoted to achieving a proper balance, keeping in mind practical feasibility and considering the following: (a) A very large (bureaucratic) organization would become unwieldy and perhaps even counterproductive; and (b) A very narrow scope for the Lokpal could reduce effectiveness, especially from the perspective of tackling corruption at the level of the common man. Therefore, deciding on the appropriate scope of Lokpal is a very critical issue, if it is to serve as an effective institution on the ground in tackling country wide corruption. It would be prudent to revisit this issue now, especially since the last decade has seen significant spectacular corruption, as noted earlier.

Third, the Lokpal must be truly independent and also be <u>seen</u> to be independent in terms of the process of the selection of its chairperson and members as well as its larger accountability as an institution. The Lokpal must, therefore, be established as a fully autonomous body capable of fulfilling the vested mandate. Under no circumstances, should the Lokpal be under the tutelage of the people/institutions who are to be investigated (by it). There should be no conflicts of interest whatsoever. The Lokpal must also be made accountable to people/institutions who do not fall under its jurisdiction. All of the above would have to apply to the Lokayuktas as well. This is a tricky issue and must be addressed—suitably during implementation—if indeed, the Lokpal is to be effective in rooting out corruption.

Last, many aspects of corruption (like bribery) call for a giver of the bribe and that calls for significant attitude change across wide sections of society in India. I hope that the Lokpal, and the associated Lokayuktas, also provide for awareness campaigns that emphasise to the public the need to refrain from giving bribes. This is perhaps the toughest task for the Lokpal as without this attitude change among the people, very little can be achieved in fighting corruption. This issue should not be underestimated because, among other things, people would be required to wait for their turn with regard to delivery of products and services and not attempt to jump the queue, when it comes to accessing various goods/services.

This is certainly a huge task in a country of over a billion people, most of whom are in a tearing hurry and willing to pay to be served out-of-turn. Alternatively, some feel a sense of entitlement by virtue of their position or status and don't think twice before using it to jump the queue. To help fix this issue on the ground, the demand-supply gap in the delivery of goods/services would also have to be reduced and unnecessary bureaucratic approvals/procedures (which are perhaps the cause of this form of bribery in the first place) eliminated. India could also look at the United Kingdom and Bhutan, which have enacted anti-bribery acts that provide disincentives and penal punishments to the bribe-giver. Let us not forget the bribe-giver in this whole matter as without them, much of the corruption would not exist.

Given the above context, restructuring of the Lokpal and Lokayukta system is very crucial to root out corruption and the associated parallel economy. It is a very necessary step required to eliminate corruption at various levels of the government, which is the bane of modern Indian society.

a) Lokpal and Lokayuktas must be truly independent bodies without any conflicts of interest so that they can be the effective tool to fight corruption of all kinds—regular as well as spectacular corruption.

b) For this, the first requirement is to make the Lokpal and Lokayuktas appropriate in terms of member composition without any conflicts of interest (CoI). Furthermore, members should have impeccable credentials and highest levels of professional and personal integrity. This would encompass taking care of political, private sector, civil service and government related conflicts of interest. This, in turn, requires a CoI subset of rules to be a part of the Lokpal and Lokayuktas legislation, and members must be mandatorily required to provide a CoI self-declaration. Furthermore, the composition of Lokpal and Lokayuktas must be decided by a broad based committee comprising heads of governments, leaders of opposition and chief justices of Supreme and High Courts along with significant participation by eminent people from civil society.

c) The Lokpal and Lokayuktas must have the jurisdiction to enquire and provide punishment to all involved in regular and spectacular corruption. The term 'all' would include politicians and civil servants, of all kinds and grades, the judiciary, constitutional and government functionaries (including Prime Minister, Chief Ministers and Ministers) and all others holding elected office including MPs and MLAs, right from the President of India to the *sarpanch* of the smallest revenue village at the local level. Additionally, all officials serving at various levels of government and in varying capacities and belonging to different categories must also come under the Lokpal and Lokayuktas, as per jurisdiction.

d) An independent body without CoI must be set up to investigate the corruption cases that get referred to and come under the jurisdiction of the Lokpal and the Lokayuktas.

e) The body must be a national level institution comprising of a broad based civil society dominant, politically neutral board. It must have a headquarters office in Delhi as well as offices in all the states. All of these offices would come under the purview of the Right to Information (RTI) act.

f) The best and most efficient, yet patriotic officers with impeccable integrity from the IPS must occupy leadership positions in such a body. The organization must also have officers of impeccable integrity, efficiency and patriotism from the Internal Revenue Service (IRS), Indian Administrative Service (IAS), Indian Foreign Service (IFS) and other services as appropriate.

g) The officers of the independent investigative organization must have all the necessary executive powers required for the investigation and solving of corruption cases. The organization's officers must report through a proper chain of command to the senior management and CEO of the institution, who in turn would apprise the board. The board will forward the extant recommendations to the respective Lokpal and/or Lokayuktas for action.

h) All officers and people involved with the Lokpal and the Lokayuktas will have to declare all assets (income, shares, jewellery etc) and file annual returns as specified in the recommendation on tax reforms given in chapter 1. The compensation provided to all the staff of this entire Lokpal and Lokayuktas setup must be in line with the best in country so that they can discharge their roles and duties without fear, favor and prejudice and in the most efficient and effective manner.

Bringing radical change in the governance of government and its institutions to eliminate corruption, enhance effectiveness and efficiency in their working and facilitate accountability in real time is a very necessary corollary as well and the Lokpal and Lokayuktas must enable this.

a) Governance of government and its institutions needs radical change. Over the last 72 years, in many instances, corruption has been rampant and arrogance has been high among those politicians holding office as well as government officials. Of course, there are several exceptions to this but across the board, the above is true and representative of many governments in India. Things have however started to change in recent times but a lot more needs to be done. Without a doubt, governments need to move to community sensitive governance and become more efficient (do things the right way), effective (do the right things) and adaptive (innovate and adapt in real time to the situation). Lokpal and the Lokayuktas must facilitate this through their regular body of work.

b) Corruption, by and large, has been rampant at all levels of government over the last 72 years because of which the prices of goods and services in the country increases consistently. Money making has become more the norm rather than the exception, especially for a government official. From getting a village officer's certificate to clearances for larger industries and/or contracts for supply of goods and services to the government, money needs to be paid out (by and large). This has to change completely and accountability must come into the system. Again, the Lokpal and the Lokayuktas must facilitate this.

c) Implementation of schemes is also poor and very little reaches the common man relative to the expenditure. Regular as well as spectacular corruption including use of middlemen for the same are key issues here and this again needs the close attention of Lokpal and Lokayuktas.

d) Middlemen have been ruling the roost for over 72 years now and as a result, the transaction costs and also (wasteful) government expenditure increases. A large amount of corruption takes place due to the presence of middlemen and the Lokpal and Lokayuktas must help tackle this menace and put an end to it, once and for all by showcasing examples of such corruption and punishing the people concerned in a serious and stringent manner.

e) While good officials exist at all levels, they are far and few relative to the corrupt group and where they resist, they are penalized. This aspect also needs attention of the Lokpal and Lokayuktas.

f) Thus, the Lokpal and Lokayuktas and their infrastructure must be strengthened to check corruption, ensure accountability and enhance efficiency and effectiveness in the delivery of government services. While an assault on corruption can achieve this, much of what is stated above needs to be closely monitored by the Lokpal/ Lokayuktas.

g) This apart, several other issues must be factored in by the Lokpal/Lokayuktas

- Reducing unnecessary government expenditure is vital to have a better economy and every department must use process mapping and value engineering to eliminate redundancy in paperwork and processes so as to reduce wasteful government activities and associated expenditure. When this is achieved, corruption will automatically come down.
- The utility of the government schemes must be continuously evaluated by an independent broad based pan India body like the CAG, which must be made completely independent of government control. It goes without saying that the appointment process of the CAG

must be made totally independent of the ruling dispensation just as in the case of the Lokpal/Lokayuktas. The recommendations so made by the CAG with regard to schemes must be implemented immediately and schemes deemed to be useless to the people must be scrapped in totality.

☞ In fact, the government must encourage entrepreneurship and move towards "minimum government and maximum governance". All unnecessary licensing and approval requirements must be streamlined to reduce the government footprint in all walks of life. This will bring down corruption significantly.

☞ A special grievances handling mechanism that automatically and independently reaches the Lokpal structure for corruption related matters and a similar one that reaches the Comptroller and Auditor General (CAG) for efficiency and effectiveness of services must be established immediately.

☞ All elected representatives occupying government office, elected representatives and government officials at all levels must come under the conflict of interest sub-rules as per the Lokpal and Lokayukta structures. Several declarations will have to be made by them while assuming office and subsequently on an annual basis. This will prevent corruption in a big way.

All of the above should reduce wasteful government expenditure and enhance efficiency and effectiveness of governance while simultaneously eliminating corruption and reducing the footprint of governments in various sectors in line with the motto, "minimum government, maximum governance".

Chapter 4

Create a Sound and Effective Public Procurement Act

Apart from a strong and independent Lokpal, a range of other aspects[148] would have to be addressed to eradicate corruption in India. The most important among these are given below:

---

[148] The other aspects are: (1) Political reforms with transparent (state and other) funding of elections which is taken up later in this book; (2) Rationalization of various taxes to encourage tax payments and facilitate better tax collections, which was addressed earlier in this book; (3) Creation of a citizen's grievance-redressal system that ensures all citizens gain access to all basic services at an appropriate cost when in need of the same; (4) Advocacy and awareness campaigns that ensure citizens commit themselves to not engaging in corrupt practices such as payment of bribes, evasion of taxes, commission of frauds, and the like; and (5) Regulation of critical sectors like financial services, to prevent fraud and corruption in public/private enterprises so as to safeguard people's money (savings), avoid over-indebtedness and the like.

a) Sound corruption-retarding policies relating to the use of natural resources such as land (and its acquisition), mining, underwater exploration, spectrum, and the like, for a variety of purposes. All of these sectors have been prone to scams, and
b) An appropriate Public Procurement Act relating to the sale/lease of natural (public) resources which have again seen the largest and biggest scams.

India is one of the few countries that does not yet have a law[149] for public procurement and in the context of the various scams that have occurred over the period 1984 to 2013, this cannot go unnoticed.[150] This, in effect, is perhaps the most important measure that the Government of India will now have to take to bring an end to corruption and the generation of black money.

Indeed, public procurement is a very large issue and goes far beyond the proposed website[151] or e-auction process[152] set up by the government. Yet, public

---

[149] A Public Procurement Bill was introduced in 2012 in Parliament but it was never enacted.
[150] Although a Public Procurement Bill, 2012 was introduced in Parliament, it never got enacted—'The Public Procurement Bill, 2012', Bill No. 58 of 2012, as introduced in the *Lok Sabha*, http://164.100.24.219/BillsTexts/LSBillTexts/asintroduced/58_2012_LS_EN.pdf
[151] An Amazon type of website is said to have been proposed for purchase of items by the government.
[152] 3 G Spectrum was e auctioned. '3G e-auction a first for India on this scale', August 04, 2008, *Livemint*, R. Jai Krishna, http://www.livemint.com/Home-

procurement has not been subject to sufficient regulation. The fact that India does not yet have a law for public procurement acquires even greater significance in the face of the multi-faceted scams that occurred especially during the period 2008 to 2013— many of these concerned public procurement of natural resources such as land, coal, mining and sale of spectrum.

In this context, I would also like to quote from the judgment handed down by Supreme Court Justice Jagdish Singh Khehar[153] in the 2G Spectrum case where he laid down that:

> **"No part of the natural resource can be dissipated as a matter of largesse, charity, donation or endowment, for private exploitation. Each bit of natural resource expended must bring back a reciprocal consideration"**[154]

In his 2015-16 budget speech,[155] the Union Minister Arun Jaitley reiterated his government's commitment to formalizing the country's public procurement

---

Page/bClR7ymFdhmAy6XG8VO5OJ/3G-eauction-a-first-for-India-on-this-scale.html

[153] Jagdish Singh Khehar was the 44th Chief Justice of India (4 January 2017 – 27 August 2017).

[154] See 'Sans 2G, Presidential Reference maintainable: court', September 28, 2012, The Hindu, J.Venkatesan, http://www.thehindu.com/news/national/sans-2g-presidential-reference-maintainable-court/article3942879.ece

[155] See 'Revamping public procurement', April 23, 2015, The Hindu, Mukul G. AsherTarun Sharma and Shahana Sheikh, http://www.thehindu.com/opinion/op-ed/revamping-public-procurement/article7130910.ece

system as a part of its continuing reforms in public financial management. In a bid to actionize the commitment, the government sought to revamp the bill framed by the previous UPA government. The bill was introduced in the last Lok Sabha by the then Finance Minister Pranab Mukherjee and referred to the Parliamentary Standing Committee on Finance in May 2012. Following no report from the Committee, the bill was allowed to lapse with the dissolution of the then Lok Sabha. The present Union Government called for feedback and suggestions on the provisions of the draft bill from civil society, non-government organizations, lawyers and industry bodies.

Some of the provisions proposed by the 2012 Bill are as follows:

- The bill[156] sought to regulate as well as ensure accountability and transparency in (public) procurement by the central government and its various entities. Procurements for disaster management and/or for security/strategic purposes were supposedly exempt from the bill. Likewise, public procurement below Rs 50 lakh was also deemed to be exempted. In addition, the government, at its discretion, was also empowered to exempt, in public interest, any procurement and/or procuring entities from the provisions of the bill.
- The government was empowered to prescribe a code of conduct and integrity for bidder and

---

[156] Paraphrased from 'The Public Procurement Bill, 2012', *PRS India*, http://www.prsindia.org/billtrack/the-public-procurement-bill-2012-2310/, **Current Status: Lapsed**

procuring entity staff and officials. Under certain circumstances, the bill also empowered the government and/or procuring entities to completely debar a bidder, if required.

- As per the mandates of the bill, all procurement-related information was to be published in a Central Public Procurement Portal in an open and transparent manner.
- Open competitive bidding was the procurement method preferred under the bill; every procuring entity had to provide reasons if it used alternative methods. Conditions and procedures were also specified for use of alternative methods of bidding.
- Procurement Redressal Committees were to be set up as per the mandates of the bill. Such committees could be approached by any aggrieved bidder for suitable remedies and redressal.
- As per the mandates of the bill, both the acceptance of a bribe by a public servant and also the offering of the same by any bidder—with a view to influencing the procurement process and outcomes—was punishable with not only a fine but also imprisonment.

Even at the time of the 2012 Bill being tabled in Parliament, there was criticism[157] about its efficacy. A number of problem areas were identified. One was the inexplicable empowerment of the government to

---

[157] See 'The Public Procurement Bill, 2012', *PRS India*, http://www.prsindia.org/billtrack/the-public-procurement-bill-2012-2310/, **Current Status: Lapsed**

exempt certain 'kinds' of procurements from the due public procurement process, and/or even to limit competition and competitive forces in specific cases. Second was the apparent reference to Open Competitive Bidding as the preferred method of procurement, even without defining the term precisely. The third was the absence of a requirement of appropriate certification by a competent technical authority (or expert) in the event of the need to source from a specific supplier, with the objective of ensuring standardization and/or enabling compatibility with existing systems. The non-restriction of the use of cost-plus contracts, which provide lesser incentive for efficiency was the fourth.

While recognizing these limitations, I would like to state that the following fundamental issues[158] should be considered while redrafting/recasting the framework proposed by the previously tabled 2012 legislation.

The first deals with transparency in public procurement. The law must ensure that there is an adequate degree of transparency in the whole (public) procurement cycle so as to facilitate fair and equitable treatment for all potential suppliers. Transparency must be maximised in competitive tendering and precautionary measures must be in place to enhance integrity, for (any) exceptions made to competitive

---

[158] This chapter draws on several resources including information from various civil society organizations, multi-lateral and bi-lateral agencies, international organizations like the Organization for Economic Co-operation and Development (OECD) and other stakeholders. They are gratefully acknowledged.

tendering (in case of urgency and/or national security).

Among other things, the law would also have to ensure the following aspects:

1. All potential suppliers/contractors must have clear and consistent information with regard to the whole procurement process and understand it well.
2. Where required, the degree of transparency may be adapted according to the recipient of information and the stage of the cycle. In other words, confidential information (trade secrets) would need to be protected to ensure a level playing field for potential suppliers, and also prevent possible collusion among stakeholders.
3. The public procurement process should be applied equitably/fairly across the entire cycle by all stakeholders and should be perceived to be fair and equitable.
4. The drive for transparency should not create unnecessary 'red tape' and inefficiency in the public procurement system, thereby causing unnecessary and huge delays.
5. Key decisions made on public procurement should be well-documented and easily accessible for examination by various stakeholders, as appropriate.
6. Relevant stakeholders (including auditors) should be able to check and determine whether specifications are unbiased and/or award decisions based on fair grounds.

7. Clear rules and concrete guidance must exist with regard to the choice of the procurement method and on exceptions to competitive tendering (if any).

All of this suggests that, for good procurement regulations, systems must not be unnecessarily complex, costly and/or time-consuming. These could cause huge delays (in the procurement) and discourage participation, especially by micro, small and medium enterprises (MSMEs).

In fact, excessive red tape in such public procurement regulations may create significant opportunities for (fresh) corruption. This would surely result in the whole purpose of enacting the legislation becoming counter-productive.

Therefore, ensuring an adequate level of transparency that enhances corruption control, while not impeding the efficiency and the effectiveness of the public procurement process, is a challenge that needs to be met by using the mantra of 'balanced enabling regulation'. I hope that the government keeps these aspects in mind while drafting the much-needed Public Procurement Act in India.

Second, the decision making process, with regard to public procurement, should be transparent in the sense of being well documented and accessible. The criteria should be clear, objective, reliable and valid, in the sense that anyone applying the said criteria will be able to come to the same (similar) judgment. This takes us to the next aspect of public procurement.

With a transparent decision making process and objective, reliable and valid criteria, it should be easy for the CAG[159] and team to revalidate the same, if required subsequently. It goes without saying that trade secrets (if any) of the participant stakeholders should be protected to prevent misuse by others.

Other aspects that such an Act should focus on include:
- Conflict of interest management of public sector and private sector officials including risks and vulnerability;
- The aspect of revolving and reverse revolving door phenomena,[160] which are the primary source of corruption also needs to be taken care by this act;
- Protection of whistleblowers;
- Internal controls to ensure that the implementation progresses as intended;
- Cycle of audits for the procurement to ensure that the funds are utilized as originally proposed and intended and also to check for action taken on reports from previous audits;
- Appropriate grievance redressal mechanisms for the suppliers and other stakeholders; and
- Empowerment of civil society organizations, media and the wider public to scrutinize public procurement.

---

[159] The Comptroller and Auditor General (CAG) of India.
[160] Please see appendix 5.

I fervently hope that these factors will be kept in mind and a freshly drafted Public Procurement Bill will be tabled in Parliament at the earliest opportunity and subsequently enacted as law.

If efforts are not made to weed out corruption, which is the fount of black money, any exercise, be it the 2016 demonetization or any other measure, would prove to be a case of addressing a superficial symptom even while leaving the root cause untouched.

Restructuring of Lokpal/Lokayuthas (as noted in chapter 3) and enacting appropriate legislation on public procurement are crucial weapons that the government needs in its armoury if it is to really win the war on corruption that it is currently waging. To be prepared is half the victory after all!

To summarize, reforming public procurement and sourcing of services/materials for government/public use in India is a very necessary and crucial aspect that needs urgent attention.

a) The Government of India must immediately pass a public procurement and services/materials sourcing act in India as public procurement and services/material sourcing has been and can be a major source of corruption. The same has to be accepted by all state legislatures and implemented in real time by the government of India and state governments.

b) The act must be comprehensive and cover extraction and sale of all natural resources (raw materials, minerals, intangible assets like spectrum etc.) in India, whether at the central or state or local government level. The same act must also be the basis for sourcing of goods and services by the government for public use—be it in infrastructure or other sectors.
c) The act must ensure complete transparency and accountability in the public procurement and services/materials sourcing processes, so that revenue from national resources and needs are at least optimized, if not maximized.
d) All public procurement must come under the audit and inspection of the Comptroller and Auditor General of India (CAG). All constitutional bodies {including the Reserve Bank of India (RBI)} as well as government and/or government aided institutions must come under a CAG audit with regards to public procurement and sourcing of services/materials for their own and public use.
e) It goes without saying that the appointment of the CAG must be streamlined and free of political and other biases and conflicts of interest. The CAG must be completely independent of the government so that an impartial, objective and candid assessment of the public procurement and goods/services sourcing processes in the entire country is possible in real time.

Thus, eliminating corruption in public procurement and goods/services sourcing is very central to building a robust economy, and the above are the most urgent tasks that need to be undertaken immediately (in conjunction with other recommendations made in this book), especially, if we desire India to witness double digit growth in the near future.

Chapter 5

Reform the Political Economy

In the earlier chapter on corruption, I had attempted to classify corruption into two kinds—regular corruption and spectacular corruption. The first kind, regular corruption, is what is experienced almost on a day to day basis—the little *baksheesh*[161] that needs to be paid to get a certificate from a public authority, to get a file 'passed', to get the traffic cop to overlook a jumped signal or to gain access to a facility/service out of turn. This kind of corruption has been institutionalized to the point where we have ceased to consider it 'bribes' or 'corrupt acts'.

The second kind most often falls in the realm of political corruption. The headline hogging scams

---

[161] https://www.merriam-webster.com/dictionary/baksheesh — "Baksheesh" is from Persian "bakhshīsh," which is also the source of the word *buckshee,* meaning "something extra obtained free," "extra rations," or "windfall, gratuity."

which cost the exchequer millions and millions of rupees, more often than not, involve those in political office. This corruption at 'the highest levels' is, after all, possible only with the tacit, if not overt, involvement of those occupying the highest echelons of power.

Political corruption is defined as the use of power by public officials for their illegitimate, private gain. While public officials include those elected/appointed to office, we will be restricting our discussion to political parties/elected peoples' representatives for the purpose of this chapter.

There are different kinds of political corruption, all of which yield personal/political gain to the elected officials. Misuse of power and office might happen for pecuniary benefit or to subvert the democratic or electoral process to win elections.

In the context of misusing power for pecuniary benefits, the beneficiaries of the political largesse are most often industrial or corporate houses. They use political donations as a tool to further short-term business interests or to establish ties[162] with political parties with an eye to long-term benefits. There are also specific instances where corporates bid for rights/licenses to commercially exploit public resources or submit tenders to meet the procurement needs of the government. In a bid to influence the public officials to award such contracts/licenses to

---

[162] This can happen through lobbying, for instance. The 'Nira Radia tapes controversy' is a case in point—see
https://en.wikipedia.org/wiki/Radia_tapes_controversy

them, commissions/cuts are offered on the total value of the said contracts to politicians in positions of power. The bribes may also take the form of land, gold, stock or other assets.

Where political donations are used as a means to lobby for legislation/public policies, the intent is to further long-term business interests. Generous donations are made to the war chests of the political parties, to finance their various electoral battles. This type of corruption could well be described as institutional corruption, since the benefit accrues to the institution or the political party in this context. Corporates/business houses/individuals bankroll the election campaigns of those political parties whose rise to power would benefit their interests. There are often instances of the same corporate house funding political parties with opposing ideologies or agendas. This is hardly surprising since the relationship with the political party is established purely to gain access to power circles rather than any significant ideological allegiance. Making payouts to multiple political parties is also a means of hedging their bets.

Some of the money that goes to line political coffers may well be legitimate, clean money. That is, the money has come through a formal financial channel, has been accounted for, and on which taxes have been paid. Some of it may take the informal route, either in the form of 'black money' hoarded within the country in the form of cash stashed away in offshore accounts. The offshore 'money' may go into the offshore accounts of persons connected with the political parties, to be routed back to India through various means, some of which may not even be legal.[163] While this would make political parties complicit in money laundering activities, the monies received thus might not be reflected in the declarations or financial statements of the political parties. In that case, they would be used to fund the 'not so above board' electoral activities like the rigging of polls by the use of muscle power, or by bribing the voters in cash or kind[164] or any other 'off-the-record' activity.

Any money paid to a political party with the intent of gaining a toehold in the corridors of power could be construed as 'dirty money', since the money is a pay-out for future benefits. Through lobbying and offering pecuniary benefits to influence the process of awarding government contracts and licenses, it goes without saying that corporate interests are gaining at the cost of public interest. It is befitting to brand the money that helps business or corporate interests triumph over public interests as 'tainted' or 'dirty' in intent.

Making political donations is not an illegal act or a crime. Such donations can and indeed often do take the form of 'clean' money routed through banking channels. Even if they do not constitute a quid pro quo in the present, like in the case of payouts for

---

[163] Most often, they come through what is called as the *'hawala'* route—See https://en.wikipedia.org/wiki/Hawala

[164] See "Cash for votes a way of political life in South India', March 16, 2011, *The Hindu,* Sarah Hiddleston, http://www.thehindu.com/news/the-india-cables/lsquoCash-for-votes-a-way-of-political-life-in-South-Indiarsquo/article14949621.ece

contracts/licenses etc., they do represent a promise for the future. The institution/political party is under an implicit obligation to serve the interests/agenda of the corporate/business house making the donation. Where large businesses and/or people with vested interests contribute to any campaign, they are bound to extract their pound of flesh eventually, if not upfront, effectively setting up a conflict of 'interests'.

Unlike the United States of America or the United Kingdom, both of which essentially have a two party system, India is a land of several political parties, espousing a mix of ideologies and sporting a range of colors. According to **Section 29B of the Representation of People's Act**[165] (RPA), 1951, each and every political party is permitted to accept voluntary contributions given to it by any person or company, other than a Government company or any local body wholly or partly financed by the Government.

Section 182 of Companies Act,[166] **2013** states two major conditions with regard to companies desirous of making contributions to political parties: 1) they must have been in existence for a minimum period of three years; and 2) they can donate, at most, 7.5 percent of their profit in a year and they are mandated to clearly identify and appropriately

---

[165] See 'The Representation Of The People Act, 1951', Act No.43 of 1951, July 17, 1951,
http://lawmin.nic.in/legislative/election/volume%201/representatio n%20of%20the%20people%20act,%201951.pdf
[166] See 'The Companies Act, 2013', (No . 18 of 2013), August 29, 2013, *Ministry of Law and Justice*, The Gazette of India,
http://www.mca.gov.in/Ministry/pdf/CompaniesAct2013.pdf

disclose the amount donated in their profit and loss account.

Furthermore, no electoral candidate, political party and/or office-bearer thereof can accept any contribution from a source defined as "foreign" under **Section 2 of the Foreign Contribution (Regulation) Act,**[167] **1976. However, an amendment to the above was made in the form of the Foreign Contribution (Regulation) Act, 2010**[168] **and this redefined the term "foreign source". As per the original provision, a foreign source** included any company with foreign investment greater than 50 percent in the Indian entity, while the amendment stated that as long as a foreign company's ownership in an Indian entity was within the (foreign investment) limits prescribed by the Government of India for that specific sector/industry, the company will be treated as "Indian" for the purposes of the FCRA.

Also, as per Section 29 C of the RPA, all registered political parties in India are mandated to submit to the Election Commission (EC) details of all donations received in excess of Rs 20,000 from any person and/or a company. This is in addition to the

---

[167] See 'Foreign Contribution (Regulation) Act, 1976', Act No. 49 of Year 1976, http://jhpolice.gov.in/sites/default/files/ForeignContributionRegulationAct_1976.pdf

[168] See 'The Foreign Contribution (Regulation) Act, 2010', No.42 Of 2010, September 26, 2010, *Ministry of Law and Justice*, The Gazette of India,http://lawmin.nic.in/ld/regionallanguages/THE%20FOREIGN%20CONTRIBUTION%20(REGULATION)%20ACT,2010.%20(42%20OF%202010).pdf

regular annual tax returns that they are required to file with the tax authorities. Here, it needs to be noted that as per Section 13A[169] of the Income Tax (I-T) Act, political parties do not have to pay any income tax on contributions received. This is, however, subject to certain specific conditions such as having the accounts audited, disclosing all details about donations received beyond the permissible limit and so on.

While Section 29C of the RPA 1951 prescribes a disclosure limit, political parties have typically been known to work their way around it. The limit laid down by the Act is to be applied to the aggregate of the various sums donated to a political party by an individual or entity or a company in a given year. The political parties have however interpreted the limit to be applicable to donations made in excess of twenty thousand rupees at one time. There are reported instances of donations being broken down into multiple contributions—each just under the permissible limit of Rs 20,000 and the donor being issued multiple receipts. It must be mentioned here that all such restrictions are applicable only to 'official' contributions made through formal banking channels.

Donations by way of cash are practically outside the purview of the Act and remain unknown and undisclosed unless the political party itself chooses to make it public. To the best of my knowledge, as on

---

[169] See 'Tax Exemption to Political Parties [Section 13A]—Income Tax', *TaxDose.com*, http://www.taxdose.com/tax-exemption-to-political-parties-section-13a-income-tax/

date, there is no law currently that completely prohibits contributions to political parties in the form of cash.[170] The only issue here is that such contributions are not eligible to be claimed as tax deductions[171] by the donors while computing their net taxable incomes.

In fact, according to the Association of Democratic Reforms[172] (ADR), the income tax returns filed by the political parties—which were obtained using the Right to Information Act (RTI)—revealed that a meagre 20 percent of the income of political parties came from contributions disclosed by them to the EC as per Section 29C. This, in effect, means that, the source is neither clearly identifiable nor established for as much as three-quarters of their income—a fact that hints at the significant cash (possibly 'black money') component in the contributions received. The ADR analysis of the total income and expenditure incurred by national parties during FY 2014-15, as declared by these parties in

---

[170] Political parties are said to have been barred from accepting cash donation beyond Rs 2,000 per individual. They can receive donations via cheques, electronic mode; electoral bonds to be issued by RBI—please see 'Jaitley lowers cash donation limit for parties to Rs 2,000', February 1, 2017, PTI, *Rediff.com*,
https://www.rediff.com/business/report/budget-jaitley-lowers-cash-donation-limit-for-parties-to-rs-2000/20170201.htm

[171] Under Sections 80-GGB and 80-GGC of the Income Tax Act, 1961, political donations made by companies and individuals are permissible as deductions while computing the net taxable income, so long as such contributions are made by way of cheque. The political party to which a donation is being made must be registered under Section 29A of the Representation of the People Act, 1951.

[172] See 'The Foreign Hand In Political Funding', October 17, 2016, *Association for Democratic Reforms (ADR)*, Indian Legal,
http://adrindia.org/content/foreign-hand-political-funding

their IT Returns submitted to the ECI, further highlights several other anomalies, including incomplete details of donors, duplicate PAN details and cheque numbers and so on.

The National Commission to Review the Working of the Constitution,[173] 2001 noted that the dire necessity for taking funds for fighting elections is the base foundation on which the whole architecture of corruption[174] rests. It has been further argued that this is a vicious cycle where the proceeds of corruption are used to fund election campaigns and the victorious campaigns, in turn, lead to more (political) corruption by subverting principles of justice, fairness and equity.

The other aspect of political corruption is that it involves the rigging of elections and subversion of the democratic process—both of which again come at a huge price. Increasingly, there is this reported trend in India of political parties bribing[175] voters in cash or kind, which in effect translates into 'buying' their way into power. According to Election Commission estimates, more than Rs 3,500 crore (approximately $750 million) was reportedly paid as a

---

[173] The National Commission to Review the Working of the Constitution was set up vide Government Resolution dated 22nd February, 2000, http://lawmin.nic.in/ncrwc/ncrwcreport.htm

[174] See 'A Consultation Paper On Review Of Election Law, Processes And Reform Options' NCRW- Final Report Book 1
http://lawmin.nic.in/ncrwc/finalreport/v2b1-9.htm

[175] See "Cash for votes a way of political life in South India', March 16, 2011, *The Hindu,* Sarah Hiddleston,
http://www.thehindu.com/news/the-india-cables/lsquoCash-for-votes-a-way-of-political-life-in-South-Indiarsquo/article14949621.ece

bribe[176] during the assembly elections in five Indian states during April-May 2011.

It is thus clearly established that there is an inextricable link between political funding, corruption and black money generation. Unless we strike at the root of corruption, the black money tree is not going to be felled. Without addressing the institutional (political) corruption that forms the base on which the superstructure is erected, corruption is not going to be uprooted.

Sam van der Staak, Programme Manager, International IDEA (an inter-governmental organization that supports sustainable democracy), has identified numerous legal anomalies in India in the context of political funding[177]. These include: a) The lack of a comprehensive election campaign finance act; b) Neither candidates nor political parties have donation or spending limits; c) Anonymous donations are banned in respect of political parties, but not candidates; d) Neither political parties nor candidates have stringent (fool proof) reporting requirements; e) State funding of elections does not exist; and f) There are no formal penalties for funding violations.

---

[176] See 'Delayed electoral reforms', January 18, 2012, *The New Indian Express,* Aditya Swarup,
http://www.newindianexpress.com/opinions/2012/jan/18/delayed-electoral-reforms-331363.html
[177] See 'The Foreign Hand In Political Funding', October 17, 2016, *Association for Democratic Reforms (ADR),* Indian Legal,
http://adrindia.org/content/foreign-hand-political-funding

At this juncture, it would be appropriate to recall the Supreme Court notice[178] to the Election Commission and the Central Government on the petition to get political parties under the Right to Information Act (RTI). The government in response[179] indicated that political parties will not be able to divulge details about their institutional functioning and financial matters under the Right to Information (RTI) Act as it would "hamper their smooth functioning" and make them vulnerable to "rivals with malicious intentions". It also pointed out that transparency on financial aspects has already been mandated and enforced under the IT Act, 1961 and the RPA, 1951.

The Election Commission (EC) has also reportedly asked the government to make graft[180] a cognizable offence during elections and has further sought to be empowered to countermand polls in the event of large scale bribery of voters. In this context, it must be recalled that in the May 2016 elections[181] to the

---

[178] See 'Parties under RTI: SC sends notice to Election Commission, Centre', July 8, 2015, *The Indian Express,* Express News Service, http://indianexpress.com/article/india/politics/supreme-court-notice-to-centre-on-plea-to-get-political-parties-under-rti/

[179] See 'Can't bring political parties under RTI, Centre tells Supreme Court', August 24, 2015, *The Hindu,* Krishnadas Rajagopal, http://www.thehindu.com/news/national/political-parties-cant-be-under-rti-act-centre-tells-sc/article7575584.ece

[180] See 'Make bribing voters a cognizable offence: Election Commission tells govt', December 4, 2016 *The Times of India,* Bharti Jain, http://timesofindia.indiatimes.com/india/Make-bribing-voters-a-cognizable-offence-Election-Commission-tells-govt/articleshow/55782208.cms

[181] See 'A first: Tamil Nadu poll cancelled over bribing voters', May 29, 2016, *The Indian Express,* Express News Service, http://indianexpress.com/article/india/india-news-india/tamil-nadu-election-commission-cancels-polls-to-two-assembly-seats-2823249/

Tamil Nadu State Assembly, the EC took the strong, bold and decisive step of countermanding the polls in two assembly constituencies following reports of large scale bribing of the electorate. This has happened subsequently[182] as well in Tamil Nadu during the 2019 general elections, when elections to the Vellore Lok Sabha seat were countermanded following the unearthing of huge amounts of cash from one of the candidates of a major political party.

The Commission is also reportedly planning a comprehensive review of the Representation of the People Act, to evaluate its ability to deal with the present day challenges and suggest suitable revisions in the form of a draft Bill. In this context, it is reported that they are considering adapting the best practices of foreign governments. For example, the Canadian law mandates that voter education be incorporated in the curriculum of educational institutions—the EC is said to be considering making a similar provision in the revised RPA.

One of the other reforms undertaken with regard to corporate donations to political parties has been the enactment of the **'Electoral Trusts Scheme, 2013'**[183] in order to streamline the process of campaign finance and also ensure the transparency

---

[182] Tamil Nadu has experienced this countermanding of elections on numerous occasions during the last decade, for the reasons mentioned above. There is general consensus that voters have been bribed by political parties and candidates, in order to win an election.
[183] See 'Functions of electoral trusts',
http://www.incometaxindia.gov.in/Rules/Income-Tax%20Rules/2008/103120000000009096.htm

with regard to corporate funding of political parties' and election expenses.

According to this scheme, Electoral Trust companies are promised tax benefits in proportion to the funds they provide to various political outfits. These companies are required to have the term 'Electoral Trust' prefixed to their names and, thereafter, be accredited under the Electoral Trusts Scheme, 2013, in order to differentiate them from companies incorporated under **Section 25 of the Companies Act, 1956.**

The companies are allowed tax benefits only if they satisfy the condition that they distribute 95 percent of total contributions received by them (in any financial year) to registered political parties within the same year itself. Furthermore, the Electoral Trust companies are not allowed to accept contributions from foreign citizens and/or overseas companies. They are also required to take the PAN number of all contributors who are resident Indians and the passport number of NRI citizens at the time of receiving the contributions.

The Electoral Trusts can possibly be compared to the Super PACs (although not in terms of incorporation) that facilitate indirect campaign finance contributions[184] by corporations to the funds of United States politicians running for office. However, Super PACs are established for specific candidates

---

[184] In the United States, direct corporate donations to individual political campaigns are forbidden.

and there are restrictions on how the funds collected can be deployed. It must be mentioned here that there is a strong movement within the United States people to abolish[185] the Super PACs system.

Electoral Bonds:[186] On January 2, 2018, the government had notified the Electoral Bond Scheme 2018. It was cited as an alternative to cash donations. The government argued that to ensure transparency in political funding, the scheme was introduced as per which, electoral bonds may be purchased by an Indian citizen and/or a company incorporated in India. As always, only political parties registered under Section 29A of the Representation of the Peoples Act, 1951 and which had secured no less than one per cent votes in the last Lok Sabha elections were eligible to receive electoral bonds, which are issued by the State Bank of India (SBI). The scheme further species that the electoral bonds can be purchased in the months of January, April, July and October and political parties are allotted a verified account by the Election Commission and all the electoral bond transactions are done through this verified account only.

The donors can buy these electoral bonds and transfer them into the accounts of the political parties as a donation. The electoral bonds are

---

[185] See 'CfA Files Federal Lawsuit Against the FEC to Abolish Super PACs', November 4, 2016, *Campaign for Accountability*, http://campaignforaccountability.org/cfa-files-federal-lawsuit-against-the-fec-to-abolish-super-pacs/
[186] See https://www.telegraphindia.com/india/electoral-bonds-explained/cid/1721437

available in denominations from Rs 1,000 to Rs 1 crore. The bonds remain valid for 15 days and can be encashed by an eligible political party only through a bank account with the authorised bank within that period only. While every donor has to provide his/her KYC details to the banks to purchase the electoral bonds, the names of the donors are kept confidential. The Communist Party of India (Marxist) and the NGO Association for Democratic Reforms (ADR) had moved the Supreme Court against the electoral bonds. The argument was that ordinary citizens will not be able to know who is donating how much to which political party. While the government argued that the privacy in electoral bonds ensures the donors privacy and also his right to vote in secret ballot, the CPI (M) had claimed that the non-disclosure of the names of the donors would add to the woes of the Indian democracy.

Late Arun Jaitley, the then Union finance minister, defended the electoral bonds and said they are aimed at checking the use of black money for funding elections, as was sought to be achieved through electoral trusts proposed during the UPA-II regime. He said in the absence of electoral bonds, donors will have no option but to donate by cash after siphoning off money from their businesses. The Supreme Court refused the Centre's submission that it should not interfere with the scheme at this stage and examine whether it has worked or not only after the ongoing general elections. The top court said it would examine in detail the changes made in laws—income tax, electoral and banking—to bring them in consonance with the electoral bond scheme and ensure the balance does not tilt in favor of any political party.

As can be seen from the above, without a doubt, the present campaign finance system in India appears to be actively fostering an environment where conflicts of interests and corruption thrive. While *'dirty money'* and a corrupt campaign finance system impede the ability to promote freedom and democracy, fight poverty, and tackle corruption, crime and terrorism, more importantly, they prevent the establishment of a *'government by the people, for the people and of the people'*.[187]

The need of the hour is a comprehensive review of existing electoral legislations. They should be revised where necessary to ensure regulation and transparency of donations made to political parties/politicians. There is also the need to make political parties accountable to the voting public, in terms of their funding sources and the purposes for which the funds are deployed.

In this regard, I would like to make the following suggestions to the EC as it contemplates comprehensive revisions to the existing The Representation of the People Act. It would be beneficial to study and adopt best practices followed in democracies the world over in this context.

---

[187] See 'The Gettysburg Address', Nicolay Copy, Gettysburg, Pennsylvania, November 19, 1863,
http://www.abrahamlincolnonline.org/lincoln/speeches/gettysburg.htm

Limits on spending: Realistically limit the extent of spending by a candidate for the office of President of India, Vice-President of India, Member of Parliament (Lok Sabha), Member of Parliament (Rajya Sabha), Member of Legislative Assembly (MLA), Member of Legislative Council (MLC) and the various candidates in local body elections. This needs to be done every five years.

Regulate funding sources: While corporate funding of elections is widely prevalent in the United States and countries of the European Union (the United Kingdom and Germany, for instance), the history and practice of corporate funding in these countries warns us of the pitfalls of excessive reliance on such donations. France leads by example in this context, having banned all political contributions from legal entities—including corporations. They place the principle of equality of candidates ahead of personal liberty in this context, not wanting to give an advantage to political parties/politicians simply by virtue of having access to larger electoral war chests. Failure to comply with both the substantive and procedural rules of election campaign financing can attract fines as well as render candidates ineligible for public office.

While I would have suggested an emulation of the French model in this context, imposing a blanket ban on corporations and companies contributing to campaign finances in India, and also imposing penalties including being rendered ineligible to contest in the event of flagrant violation of the rules, given the reforms suggested in the earlier chapters, it would be prudent to permit the funding of elections through political action committees.

However, here, we must keep in mind that today, much[188] of the campaign finance comes from powerful corporate interests and it must be emphasized that there is no free lunch. For example, the finance, real estate, insurance and several other industries—that have a keen interest in legislation—have contributed significantly in the past. Candidates for office feel obliged to tap into the currency chests of these special interests in order to get their messages out and run competitive campaigns.

Although there is a cap on corporate donations as prescribed by the Companies Act, 2013, laws are circumvented by making contributions in cash and other forms (often constituting the black money component of campaign donations) that fly under the EC's radar.

The only major alternative is to self-fund, which many people cannot afford. An electoral system that relies on candidates to be either super-wealthy or pander to powerful special interests in order to fundraise is effectively broken. A better system would be to publicly finance viable candidates. This would permit candidates who have received a qualifying number of small contributions to receive public financing for their campaigns, making them

---

[188] See 'Who funds political parties? 90 percent of donations in 2013-2014 came from corporates', December 25, 2014, *Firstpost*, FP Staff, http://www.firstpost.com/politics/funds-political-parties-90-percent-donations-2013-2014-came-corporates-2015067.html

accountable only to the general public and not to special interests.

Senior journalist M.K. Venu, in a published article, even makes a case[189] for "the Centre to consider levying a cess, or tax, for the purpose of funding political parties and the elections." He argues that even if a minuscule tax of 0.5 percent of GDP is collected over five years from corporates and high net worth individual tax payers, a corpus of about Rs 60,000 crore will become available for the Election Commission to administer as a constitutional body. His rationale is that, if such funds are put in a common pool controlled and regulated by the EC, the probability of direct deal—making between big companies and political parties stands minimizsed. Under such circumstances, the Election Commission can itself monitor the acquisition of airtime on national broadcast channels, to enable the political parties to make their 'pitch' to the voting population. This would completely obviate the need for huge expenditure on various broadcast and outdoor media to drive home their 'political messages'.

Action against voter bribery: Make bribery a cognizable offense before, during and after an electoral campaign with suitable deterrents for the voting public too. The voting public especially need to be made to understand that they are 'selling' themselves cheap, since the election eve bribes make

---

[189] See 'Time to Institutionalise Funding of Political Parties', April 17, 2016, *The Wire,* M.K. Venu, http://thewire.in/29984/time-to-institutionalise-funding-of-political-parties/

politicians feel entitled to the 'powers and privileges' that they have 'paid' for as well as eliminate any sense of accountability to the voting public until the dawn of the next electoral cycle.

Perks and benefits: Bar candidates from accepting perks and privileges, like the use of corporate jets for example, during the campaign process.

Eliminate cash donations: Mandate that all contributions to individual candidates and political parties occurs through banking channels. Stipulate that contributions to individual candidates and political parties to be made digitally. At most, limit the cash donations to Rs 500 only.

Maintenance of public database: Facilitate the creation and maintenance of a database, which is a compendium of all the above information (on the lines of the database maintained by the Federal Election Commission (FEC) in the United States in its site www.fec.gov), within one month of the monies having been received by the candidates. There will have to be regular filings once a person has announced his/her candidature. This would ensure transparency as envisaged by the RPA and impose a sense of accountability even without political parties falling under the ambit of the RTI.

The American model is worthy of emulation here, also because there are strict public disclosure legislations for both federal candidates and Political Action Committees (PACs). Donations by corporations to political parties are disclosed by respective political parties and disseminated by the media to ensure greater public awareness.

To sum it up, political (institutional) corruption is established to be the base on which the entire super structure of illegal money, nepotism, vested interests and exploitation rests. If the professed goal of culling black money from the economy, is to be achieved, it is imperative to strike at the roots. Unless the base of political corruption is shaken, the edifice of black money will not crumble. A mere crack or two can be plastered over in no time. Rather than chipping away at the cracks to get them to widen, it would benefit the economy to detonate the base and bring the structure down in its entirety. It is hoped that the political parties will treat the rot within the system rather than restricting their focus to the symptoms alone.

Accordingly, the following re-engineering of the political economy is suggested to eliminate corruption and have a vibrant democracy so vital for a strong, resilient economy. This is one of the key tasks before us. There are several recommendations in this regard:

a) First concerns the political processes. Much of the malaise that arises from the political economy is the lack of alternatives. The first step required is for the political system to create choices. That can only be done by limiting the number of terms for any person in an elected position to a maximum of two terms, irrespective of the political office. This will go a long way in promoting choice, reducing dependence on personality oriented politics and eliminating corruption. There can, however, be no restrictions on party positions. Also, candidates with proven criminal records and convictions cannot contest elections. Those with ongoing criminal cases (that are neither politically motivated nor fall under activist demonstration cases) cannot contest until their cases are over and/or a no objection is provided by the competent court.

b) Every election requires a candidate to spend money and this is the root cause of corruption. This needs serious reforms. What is proposed is as follows:

  i. State funding of elections where by a Lok Sabha Member of Parliament (MP) will get Rs 5 crore, Rajya Sabha MP will get Rs 50 lakh, an MLA will get Rs 2 crore and so on as may be decided by the election commission in consultation with the key stakeholders. A total of Rs 50000 crore can be spent on election expenditure per election cycle. Candidates who meet certain criteria alone (to be framed by the CEC after a nationwide consultation) will be eligible for state election funds. Those who receive state election funds must submit daily expenses to the central election commission (CEC) with a one-week time lag at maximum.
  ii. Candidates will be allowed to form Political Action Committees (PACs), which can collect

and spend money for and on behalf of political parties and candidates. PACs will have to be body corporates and can function nationally, state wise and at local level. They have to be registered with the central election commission (CEC) and follow forms norms and rules of the CEC which would include daily reporting of their expenditure to the CEC, with a maximum time lag of seven days. PACs will have restrictions on the amount they can spend per candidate. PACs will be subject to strict CAG AUDIT and also CEC audits to prevent diversion of money—e.g. bribing of voters which is an aspect that has become very common in India, especially during the last decade. PACs WILL also have to file annual returns. All monies received by PACs will be subject to a 25 percent election tax at the receiver's end which will go into the CECs pool of funds. It is believed that the above would play a huge role in enabling state funding of elections. Coupled with the earlier measures on taxation and other reforms regarding corruption, state funding of elections should enhance transparency and accountability in the electoral system.

c) Apart from b i) and ii) above, candidates cannot spend any money on elections.

d) All monies contributed over Rs 500 will have to be paid digitally.

e) Candidates will not be allowed to bribe or pay voters for their votes. Anyone caught doing this or contravening any of the above norms will be debarred from contesting any election for life. Additionally, severe punishments in terms of life sentences of up to 10 years may also be considered as bribing of voters is a very serious offence.

It is believed that if the above reforms are carried out, corruption, the bane of Indian politics, will disappear and we can have a healthy democracy contributing to a healthy economy as well, which can grow at double digit rates, provide greater employment and reduce poverty and inequality as well.

Chapter 6

Conclusion

The Indian economy is at a crossroads. GDP growth was at around 4.5 percent in the last quarter. The state of the economy, despite the stimulus packages offered by the finance ministry and GoI, continues to be dismal. What is called for is a set of interrelated radical steps on several fronts to ramp up the economy. Manufacturing clusters in many towns are in the doldrums and clearly, India is in the grip of a deep recession.

While the above may be the facts of the case, much of the blame for this has to lie on the governance of the past 72 years (from 1947) where corruption, crony capitalism and extreme non-friendly business practices permeated the environment. While it may be easy to point fingers at demonetization and implementation of the GST for the present state of affairs, this may neither be fair nor just. Much of the problems lie in the decades long strong misgovernance where corruption, nepotism and many other ills reared their ugly head. Thus, cleaning up of this mess was completely necessary and that is what one hugely important event in the last five years, i.e. demonetization, attempted to do on November 8, 2016.

The stated objectives of the demonetization exercise were the flushing out of the unaccounted and/or black money and counterfeit notes from the economy. While it can be described as a war on terrorism in the context of the latter, the former is a bit more complex. This is because the Indian economy has been predominantly cash driven, with an entire parallel economy in place.

Even though the incomes of a good majority of people subsisting in the parallel economy fall within the tax exemption limit prescribed by the authorities, the money still falls into the unaccounted category. This is because the monies from this parallel economy are not routed through the formal banking channels.

At this juncture, it is important to make a crucial distinction between black money, which traditionally has the connotation of being a byproduct of illegal or unlawful transactions, and the unaccounted money of the small producers, artisans, service providers, MSMEs, etc., in the parallel economy. Black money is thus only a part of, and not all of, the currency that is circulated through the parallel economy.

It goes without saying that integration of the parallel economy with the formal economy would generally be a positive consequence, since it would make available increased resources for growth and development initiatives. All other issues notwithstanding, it must be admitted that but for demonetization, the process of integrating money from the parallel economy with the formal banking system would not have really started. Multiple strategies adopted to achieve absorption of the cash circulating in the parallel economy into the banking system have failed, owing to a variety of reasons. Demonetization, in 2016, has achieved this objective to some extent and it is a great beginning. No pain, no gain is an oft quoted maxim. However, it must be said that pain could have been mitigated and its management better achieved in the context of demonetization.

Among the questions that now lie before us is how permanent has the effect of demonetization been in terms of rooting out black money. For example, while it has certainly succeeded in routing the currency floating in the parallel economy at a specified point of time into the formal banking system, the question remains as to whether this will be a one-off effect or if it will result in a more permanent attitudinal and behavioral change in the economy. Sadly, an answer to this question suggests that while demonetization did achieve in bringing a significant proportion of the parallel economy into the banking sector, much of it seems to have gotten back to where it originally was—i.e. transacting outside of the banking system. Furthermore, still, there is also the urgent need to bring back black money stashed away as cash in offshore bank accounts in tax havens or as real estate acquisitions in foreign lands.

Thus, while the demonetization exercise arm twisted many people and entities into joining the mainstream to protect the value of their cash reserves in demonetized currency, the formal system has not been able to retain its complete hold on this fresh clientele. While much depends on how the formal financial systems, whether it is the banks or the digital financial service providers, respond to the opportunity ahead of them, it is certainly no easy task to break the centuries-old obsession with cash, which is still the most flexible and convenient method of making transactions, at least from a low-income person's perspective.

On the flip side, though, the fallout of demonetization has left a lasting impact on the common man's psyche, pretty much ensuring that he is never going to feel the same about cash. This is not surprising, because what he thought of as his most liquid asset ceased to be fungible in the open market overnight, leaving him with no option but to deposit/exchange it within the formal financial system. Memories of the hardships associated with the process won't go away in a hurry, so deep is the impact. In hindsight and in the wake of the huge implementation related issues, one is forced to wonder about the degree of preparedness of our economic system to absorb such a seismic shift.

Efficiency levels have come under question as also the ability to anticipate and second guess the motives of those forces that are opposed to any move to cleanse the economy of corruption. Corruption is so deep-rooted and so deeply entrenched within the institutional hierarchy that some of those entrusted with the task of cleansing the system have themselves colluded with the 'corrupt forces'. It has been disconcerting to read of the complicity[190] of officials even within the central banking authority, not to mention the banking officials,[191] in enabling 'corrupt forces' to get their demonetized notes exchanged or to gain access to freshly minted notes, overriding the legitimate needs of the larger population.

A critical learning from the demonetization process has been the need to strengthen the system's preparedness in dealing with macro-level changes at short notice and the meticulous planning that perforce needs to precede the same. While some glitches are excusable given the mammoth size of the task, it has to be said that there were some glaring planning errors that ought to have been avoided. For example, the resizing of the newly minted two thousand rupee note is inexplicable, given the

---

[190] See 'Demonetisation: RBI official, JDS leader in CBI net', December 13, 2016, *The Economic Times,* PTI, http://economictimes.indiatimes.com/news/politics-and-nation/senior-rbi-official-arrested-for-illegal-currency-exchange/articleshow/55957443.cms

[191] See 'Demonetisation: 27 public sector bank officials suspended over corrupt practices, 6 transferred', December 2, 2016, *Firstpost,* PTI, http://www.firstpost.com/india/demonetisation-27-public-sector-bank-officials-suspended-over-corrupt-practices-6-transferred-3136880.html

resultant need for recalibration of thousands of ATMs, a task that further delayed the process of issuing fresh currency to replace the SBNs.

Second, the issuance of 2000 rupee notes alone as a replacement for the SBNs in the immediate aftermath of demonetization further queered the pitch, with a lot of people refusing to accept the note as they did not have sufficient change to offer in return, especially when the purchases were for less than five hundred rupees. A more judicious mix of denominations could have been adopted and this might have reduced the hardship brought about by 'lack of change'. This apart, the 2000 rupee note made it easier for the hoarders of black money to easily stash their black money away, as has been espoused by the many subsequent events (i.e. income tax raids) in the years following the 2016 demonetization.

Third, as pointed out earlier, the delivery mechanisms should have been trained to react with greater alacrity. Additionally, alternate mechanisms[192] better equipped to handle the scale of service and at the required speed should also have been deployed. I would like to believe that the planning bodies and those in charge of execution would be treating this as

---

[192] Here, given the currency crisis created by demonetization, one wonders whether the Indian Army could have been used to supply currency to various banks and ATM's. The Indian Army is well-known for its ability to manage crisis situations and their integrity is beyond questioning. I am sure that they would have accomplished the task in a much better fashion as compared to the private cash operators, who are prone to corrupt practices at times.

a learning experience and drawing lessons from it, despite the considerable economic and human cost.
Even while acknowledging the problems associated with the process, **I feel it appropriate to re-emphasize the central theme of this book, which is the need for a forward looking approach to ensure that we maximize the efforts to overcome the current slowdown in the Indian economy.**

Without a doubt, the need of the hour is to jump-start the economy by putting purchasing power back in the hands of the people and by pumping sufficient capital into infrastructure building to generate large scale employment opportunities. *These are broad prescriptions of course and I offer below a short list of the specific recommendations*[193] *made in earlier chapters.*

1A. Abolish income tax and introduce a banking transaction tax

If the mythical bogeyman struck terror in our hearts while we were children, the all too real taxman strikes fear in our hearts even after we are all grown up. Not even the most honest and upright amongst us can claim to have a particular affinity for the species. The farther away they are, the greater at peace we are. And yet, their tentacles reach out and ensnare us all the time, in ways that we sometimes don't even notice. Then there are the times when we feel that we are directly under their microscopic scrutiny, like

---

[193] The rationale for these recommendations can be found in the respective chapters given earlier.

cornered organisms that lie trapped under their gaze. Either which way, there is no hope of escape.

Why such an aversion to the taxman, though, and why the desperation to get away from their scrutiny? Why do the palms of even the mightiest amongst us sweat in their presence? It is obviously because the taxman's job is to take away from us a portion of our hard earned money. Their justifications of common good simply don't convince us but we are not empowered to resist.

Clearly, people didn't enjoy paying taxes back then, just as they don't today. When more and more people find ways to evade the taxman by not bringing their income/wealth or a portion of it into the books, such unaccounted monies slowly accumulate and fuel a whole new parallel (shadow) economy that subsists alongside the formal economy. No portion of the income derived from it is contributed to state expenditure on 'common good'.

Like their counterparts in history, most governments choose tax raids and punitive justice as the weapons to be unleashed on such hoarders of cash. The Government of India chose the not so commonly used weapon of demonetization, for the third time in the last seventy-two years. The stated objective, of course, was noble and to slay the demon of black money, along with lesser demons like counterfeit currency and bring to light the 'underground economy' that had remained under the spell of the 'black money' demon. While the idea of demonetization was an excellent one, it was only the beginning and more has to be done as black money still rules the roost. Clearly, we need an alternative approach and one that will be effective in rooting out black money once and for all. That is not all. **We need to find an effective mechanism, without taxing the common man, to fund government expenditure and also enhance domestic savings and consumption, boost exports and the like.**

So what is to be done?

a) A crucial step here is to abolish all direct taxes—i.e. personal income tax and corporate tax including all kinds of capital gains tax (both short and long term). Corporate tax will also be abolished for all body corporates including trusts, societies and the like. The same will be substituted with a banking transaction tax (BTT) of 75 paise per every Rs 100. Based on FY 2018-19 data, this BTT would have facilitated revenue collection[194] to the tune of Rs 21.65 lakh crore[195] as against a direct tax collection of Rs 11.37 lakh crore.

As the velocity of the banking transactions increase, the BTT would also be good enough to cover any potential deficits in the indirect taxes (whose reform is given below) and perhaps even help in eliminating these totally as well. The BTT

---

[194] See appendix 1 and 1a.
[195] For FY 2018-19, the total value of RBI payment system transactions stood at Rs 28,86,465 billion, which is Rs 28,86,46,500 crore (1 billion Rs = Rs 100 crore). If we compute a BTT of Rs 0.75 per Rs 100 across this Rs 28,86,46,500 crore flowing through the payment system, we get a BTT collection of Rs (28,86,46,500 crore x 0.75)/100 which equals Rs 21,64,849 crore or Rs 21.65 lakh crore.

should ultimately settle down at 50 paise per Rs 100, once the system stabilizes. The BTT is what I see as a fair system to taxation, without burdening the common person—it will bring into its fold, almost everyone in the country from a tax perspective. Currently, less than 10 percent of India is part of the direct tax system.

b) Another crucial step is to demonetize the following currency—Rs 2,000, Rs 500, Rs 200 and Rs 100. Meanwhile, prior preparation is required to step up digital capacity in the country in terms of more ATMs and enhance effectiveness of the cash management system in existing ATMs. Furthermore, there are many low income people who lack the digital and process literacy to be seamlessly integrate into the transforming, digitally oriented economy. They have to be assisted significantly so that they are not left behind. The various key measures required to achieve this are outlined in appendix 1c.

Money supply must also be significantly enhanced in terms of new Rs 200, Rs 100 and Rs 50 notes. This implies that large currency will be done away with altogether. All logistics must be worked out properly to avoid the problems faced in the demonetization exercise of 2016. The demonetized currency can be used for emergency services with a logistically managed cut-off date—this is to ensure that there is no hardship for the people at large.

c) People must be given 120 days to deposit all of their cash held in the form of the above currencies (that would have ceased to be legal tender as on the date of demonetization, barring the exception of use for emergency services immediately). **Likewise, all people with illegal deposits in banks abroad would also be able to bring in their money as long as pay a BTT of Rs 10 per Rs 100.** It is estimated[196] that between $216-$500 billion of illegal Indian money lies abroad in overseas bank accounts. Assuming the actual is at least mid-point, we can reasonably peg the volume of illegal foreign money at a conservative $300 billion.

No questions are to be asked regarding the source of money as long as the cash is deposited in the bank or money is transferred to the bank from overseas. A BTT of 75 paise for every Rs 100 would be charged on all cash deposits within India (post demonetization) and Rs 10 per Rs 100 would be charged on all illegal foreign inward remittances.[197] After the illegal foreign inward remittances have come in and been lodged in the

---

[196] See 'Indians' unaccounted wealth abroad estimated at $216-490 billion: Studies', June 24, 2019, PTI, https://economictimes.indiatimes.com/news/economy/finance/indians-unaccounted-wealth-abroad-estimated-at-216-490-billion-studies/articleshow/69928218.cms?from=mdr and Wikipedia https://en.wikipedia.org/wiki/Indian_black_money

[197] As noted above, assuming that $ 300 billion of Indian illegal money lies abroad and given a BTT of Rs 10 on Rs 100, we can expect a total onetime revenue inflow of Rs 2.03 lakh crore, which can serve as the core corpus for state funding of elections discussed later.

bank account (subject to a BTT of Rs 10 per Rs 100 for the first time), subsequent transactions will attract a BTT of Rs 75 paise for every Rs 100.

Thus, all rotating funds in the payment system (as defined by the RBI) will be subject to a BTT of 75 paise for every Rs 100. While cash deposits would attract a BTT of 75 paise per Rs 100, cash withdrawals would attract a BTT of Rs 1.25 per Rs 100, beyond a limit of Rs 30 lakh per quarter. Otherwise, cash withdrawals will entail a BTT of 75 paise per Rs 100. When transfers occur between two accounts owned by the same person occurs, BTT would be 50 paise per Rs 100. Other account transfers within a family would incur a BTT of 60 paise per Rs 100. All other account transfers would attract a BTT of 75 paise per Rs 100. Current account transfers would have a BTT of Rs 1 per Rs 100.

d) While income tax would have been abolished, income, property/assets (including shares) and jewellery status returns would have to be filed at the end of the 120 days (after the demonetization exercise) so that any future sales of assets can be ensured to be through the bank only. Also, the veracity of income sources to prevent future accumulation of black money can be ensured.

e) The income tax department can be downsized and rationalized in terms of work and functions as required by the above. Redeployment of staff in other suitable departments and positions would also need to be done.

f) Anyone found contravening the spirit and character of this genuinely positive and forward looking strategy will face prosecution and severe action provided they are found: (i) to have the demonetized notes after the 120 day period; and (ii) to be hoarding legal currency, beyond the prescribed limit of Rs 10 lakh per quarter. This means that, at most, at any time, this is the maximum permissible amount that can be found with any person/entity, subject to the condition that the quarter cash withdrawals don't exceed Rs 30 lakh.

The above will turbo-charge domestic consumption, enhance domestic savings, reduce interest rates for lending and make exports competitive apart from helping to generate funds for development including infrastructure, enhance investment and transform India into a rapidly growing economy. It will also enhance the size of the economy, especially, given that the parallel (black) economy and informal sector would have been fully absorbed into the mainstream. Under these circumstances, in the medium term, growth rates are expected to exceed 15 percent and this is genuinely feasible and possible.

1B. Rationalize the GST and indirect tax system

The GST will have to be rationalized and the GST council must have a good level of public representation so that issues from the field are communicated in real time. The GST slabs must be eliminated and we must move towards a single national rate for GST with key essential items exempted from GST. The operationalization of the GST including its simplification is discussed below:

Furthermore, the following reforms will be required with regard to The Goods and Services Tax (GST)[198] system. This is very necessary to put India firmly on the double digit growth path. Several steps are required in this regard:

a) Reconstitute the GST council with sufficient representation for the civil society. Again, as in the case of the Lokpal and the Lokayuktas, the GST council must also be governed by a comprehensive conflict of interest rules to prevent corruption. The GST council must also reflect enhanced sensitivity to all kinds of MSMEs, agro enterprises and the like.

b) Rationalize the GST list, exempt essential items and implement a single national rate of 5 percent. This can be done by the reconstituted GST council.

c) Simplify compliances and reduce them to a minimal. Use value engineering to optimize the filing of GST returns and compliances, which should ideally be one form per month.

---

[198] See 'Goods and Services Tax (GST) Bill, explained', October 19, 2016, The Indian Express, Express News Service, http://indianexpress.com/article/explained/gst-bill-parliament-what-is-goods-services-tax-economy-explained-2950335/

d) The reforms in direct taxes and associated processes and BTT should ensure fool proof collection of the GST via the banking channels as the scope for black transactions would have been completely eliminated. Additionally, the BTT as well as the high velocity of rotation of money through the banks (which should further enhance the BTT), should offset any potential loss in collection of the GST from previous levels.[199] Also, with burgeoning growth of the economy, GST, in reality, should reach record collections.

e) Completely exempt exports from purview of GST. Streamline filings and permissions in this regard. Again returns should be one page at the most.

f) A key final issue in the implementation of the GST framework is the distribution of GST revenue to the states. There is a long lead time before this money reaches the states. This has to change and an amendment introduced so that any GST accrual to the states reaches them, with a lag time of two weeks (at the maximum).

All of this should again contribute towards building a healthy and vibrant indirect tax system that should again fuel the economy to grow at rates greater than 15 percent.

---

[199] Based on FY 2018-19 data, the proposed BTT of Rs 0.75 per Rs 100 would have facilitated revenue collection to the tune of Rs 21.65 lakh crore as against a direct tax collection of Rs 11.37 lakh crore. In fact, the BTT collection, as stated above, would be more than sufficient to compensate fully for the total of indirect taxes as well which totaled Rs 9.39 lakh crore in FY 2018-19.

2. **Reduce stamp duty and registration fees for land registration to 1 percent (at the maximum) and increase land guideline values to be in line with land market values.**

Simultaneously, in the realty sector, stamp duty and registration fees for property and other documents must be rationalized.

Specifically, the state governments must be made to increase guideline values in urban, peri-urban and rural areas so that they are in line with market values. Rules of thumb to be used for the same were discussed earlier. Stamp duty and registration must be reduced to 1 percent of the registered document value—this is to take care of administrative and other expenses. The increase in guideline values will ensure no loss to the state government exchequer. This way black money in real estate would be eliminated and much of that money will flow into the formal economy.

Again, no questions will be asked on property registration as long as proof of RTGS or bank payment for full registered document value from buyer to seller is included. Further specific aspects are provided in the relevant chapter. Again, a point to note here is that not all cash is black and not all black is cash and suitable steps have to be taken to eliminate other sources of black money and incentivize people and corporations such that this money finds itself into the banking system, so that the very nominal charge of BTT can be levied as specified above.

The case for the above gets strong if one considers a Finance Ministry report in 2012, which noted that real estate is said to account for almost 50 percent[200] of the black money market. The real estate sector has a certain opacity factor that allows black money invested within to remain hidden, even while in plain sight. What this essentially means is that even while the black money is manifested in the form of the asset, making for a significant portion of its market value in fact, it remains invisible in terms of the property 'document' value.

The scope for undervaluing property in official documentation is what makes real estate the most sought after choice of the black money hoarders. The property guideline values in the land revenue registers of the revenue authorities are outdated and have not been aligned with market values in many years. So, people can easily get away with registering properties at a fraction of the market value, with only the guideline value, reflected in the property sale deed,[201] being settled through a banking transaction—the remaining is usually paid in the form of black money.

While real estate deals are indeed a preferred means to camouflage unaccounted cash reserves by converting them to a fixed asset, the physical cash merely changes hands. The velocity of money then comes into play as it passes through numerous hands

---

[200] See 'The Un-real Estate: The sector that is going to take the biggest hit', November 13, 2016, *The Indian Express,* Smita Nair, http://indianexpress.com/article/india/india-news-india/the-un-real-estate-demonetisation-process-100-500-rupee-note-narendra-modi-black-money-4372286/
[201] This is typically the guideline value set by the state government.

in its travel through the economy, multiplying manifold the levels of tax evasion. More often than not, the cash component of a real estate deal is higher than the property 'document' value that is settled through a banking transaction.

Given the critical role of the real estate sector in contributing to GDP growth, and also its role as the second largest employment generator, the sector's well-being is crucial to the health of the larger economy. In 2013 itself, the then Chairman of the Confederation of Real Estate Developers Associations of India, Pradeep Jain, called for reforms[202] to the sector, considering how critical the sector was for the Government to achieve (reasonable) growth targets of even 7-8 percent per annum. The sector is said to impact more than 250 manufacturing and services industries including steel and cement. Apart from industry level concessions, tax rebates and project finance, certain other concessions need to be extended to ensure the health of the sector in the interest of the investors as well as the economy.

The above apart, what is critical is an immediate rationalization of guideline values[203] of properties in the revenue department records, making them more in tune with the actual rates that prevail in the markets. Even where parties to a transaction are

---

[202] See 'Reforms in real estate key to GDP growth: Credai', January 6, 2013, *The Hindu Business Line,*
http://www.thehindubusinessline.com/news/real-estate/reforms-in-real-estate-key-to-gdp-growth-credai/article4279859.ece

[203] This needs to be undertaken by the respective state governments.

willing to record the entire sale value,[204] they are often dissuaded by the revenue officials themselves on the grounds that it would set a precedent and prove a deterrent to other parties wanting to avail themselves of the benefits of low property guideline values. A rationalization of the property guideline values with the prevailing market rates would force the transacting parties to register the sale at actual cost rather than a fraction of it, thereby eliminating the black money component in the transaction. That is the key point that needs to be noted here. And with rationalization, it would become next to impossible for the sector to absorb black money the way it is doing currently.

A rule of thumb can be applied for correcting the property guideline value—increase the guideline value by 5 to 6 times for rural areas, 3 to 4 times for peri-urban areas and 2 to 3 times for urban areas. As someone with grassroots level experience across the country, this is a simple heuristic I suggest to arrive at initial estimates for revising the guideline value. These can subsequently be adjusted as per actual demand.

Stamp duties and registration charges are the other important components in any real estate transaction and they too need to be rationalized[205] across India

---

[204] In many cases, the seller is ready to accept all money via the bank but the buyers are reluctant because they cannot show a proper source for the monies provided. This then forces legitimate tax abiding sellers also to accept black (unaccounted) money.
[205] See 'Slash stamp duty to clean up real estate sector: Assocham', November 14, 2016, *The Economic Times,* PTI, http://economictimes.indiatimes.com/wealth/real-estate/slash-

to further eliminate the black money component. Both these revenue receipts accrue to the individual states and the Central government has no jurisdiction over them.

Since stamp duty and registration fees are calculated as a percentage of the total value of the transaction, rationalizing guideline values will result in a huge increase in the transaction costs related to any property purchase. Since it is incumbent on the buyer to pay stamp duty and registration fees, he would prefer to undervalue the consideration quoted in the deed of sale to save on the costs of stamp duty and registration charges. The current stamp duty rates range[206] from as low as 4 percent to as high as 10 percent.

The National Housing Bank, which is a subsidiary of the RBI, must work along with IG of Registrars in different states to rationalize and reduce stamp duties. At no point or in no state should stamp duty and registration fees be in excess of 1 percent of the guideline value in line with the best practices the world over. As noted earlier, there would be gain rather than loss to the state exchequer if guideline values approximate market values, even with the above (low) stamp duties and registration charges.

In the current situation of unrealistic guideline values and exorbitant stamp duty charges, people will resort

---

stamp-duty-to-clean-up-real-estate-sector-assocham/articleshow/55413511.cms?from=mdr

[206] A listing of stamp duty rates across states is provided in the appendices in the book.

to undervaluing the properties to avoid paying taxes and this will only result in a loss to the exchequer. This will also have a cascading effect[207] since the transaction value will have a direct bearing on other taxes like property tax, wealth tax and gift tax.

A recursive cycle will be set off where, in order to avoid revealing the existence of this black money, the individual or the company must utilize it in ways that maintain secrecy. The monies derived from undervaluation/evasion cannot be brought into the books of accounts and hence cannot be used for legitimate or official transactions. Such monies accumulated through such unaccounted means produce a cascading effect through the entire production process, as activities must continue to remain hidden. Put differently, the underreporting incentive in property sale and stamp duties feeds the "black economy" by driving more such unaccounted money and resources into the sector, which then multiplies even further as it is used to fuel a variety of transactions in the black or the parallel economy.

For example, the most frequent recipients of the unaccounted funds would be property builders who, in turn, will continue to have incentives to circulate this unaccounted cash in the parallel (black) economy. And the further this money circulates, it fuels a whole range of other transactions that fall out

---

[207] See 'Stamp Duties in Indian States: A Case for Reform', September 2004, *World Bank Policy Research Working Paper 3413*, James Alm, Patricia Annez, and Arbind Modi, http://documents.worldbank.org/curated/en/775111468750283848/pdf/WPS3413.pdf

of the ambit of the tax system. For example, cash payments to raw materials suppliers earlier resulted in loss of sales tax and excise duties—now, loss of GST. Likewise, property builders who receive the payments as cash avoid showing these receipts as income and hence, evade income tax. Taken together, all these recipients of the unaccounted black (cash) money start the cycle of buying goods and services in the black economy, all of which continue to escape the tax net with a huge cascading effect. The net result is that not only are stamp duty and registration fees avoided, but a whole range of taxes are lost both by the central and state governments. Also, black attracts more black in the sense that the scope for undervalued transactions and tax evasion thereon attract more and more people who are looking for ways to 'unofficially' invest their unaccounted for wealth.

Effectively, if rationalization of guideline values and stamp duty charges happens, it directly eliminates the scope for a black money component in real estate transactions, since there is no scope to conceal or evade, especially if personal income and corporate taxes are abolished.

In the wake of demonetization, it was thought that it would be extremely difficult to structure real estate deals with a black money component. It was considered that the reserves lost then might take time to build them up all over again, except for what might have already been routed out of the country to be brought back through other means.

However, if we look at what is happening in real estate in India in 2019, the same trend of registering at low guideline values has continued and a significant proportion of the land registration is taking place with a huge black money component.[208]

And state governments have played a role in perhaps unknowingly encouraging this by enhancing the stamp duties and reducing the guideline values further when they should have implemented the reverse instead (lower stamp duties and higher guidelines values).

The case of Tamil Nadu, where stamp duty and registration fees have been increased from 8 percent (7 percent + 1 percent) to 11 percent (7 percent + 4 percent) coupled with a reduction in guideline values by almost 1/3rd the previous value[209] is a great example of how and why black money in real estate refuses to go away.

---

[208] This is based on my travels and experience across India both before and after November, 2016.

[209] See 'Tamil Nadu has second highest property registration cost among states', July 13, 2019, Jayaraj Sivan, The Times of India, https://timesofindia.indiatimes.com/city/chennai/tn-has-2nd-highest-property-regn-cost-among-states/articleshow/70199925.cms
See 'Guideline value cut by 33% in T.N.', June 8, 2017, Dennis S. Jesudasan, https://www.thehindu.com/news/national/tamil-nadu/tn-government-slashes-guideline-value-by-33/article18853030.ece
See 'Circular to Public', Registration Department, Government of Tamil Nadu, http://www.tnreginet.net/circular/public_Circulars/Circular_Guideline_Reduction_RF_Revision.pdf

The above has to change and in the realty sector, stamp duty and registration fees for property and other documents must be rationalized as outlined below:

a) At no time, should stamp duty and registration fees[210] exceed 1 percent of total property guideline value (GV) which must also be increased as per the following rules of thumb:
   - ☞ increase existing GV by 5 to 6 times in rural areas;
   - ☞ increase existing GV by 3 to 4 times in peri urban areas; and
   - ☞ increase existing GV by 2 to 3 times in urban areas;

b) The assistance of the National Housing Bank, a subsidiary of RBI, can be taken in this regard and a national level database created with regard to land guideline values across the various states of India. This has to be updated on a regular, at least annual basis so that guideline values are in line with market values.

---

[210] No loss to the exchequer is expected from this downward revision of stamp duties and registration fees to 1% as property guideline values would have been commensurately increased to reflect true market values. Also, the BTT component, as proposed in this book, is Rs 0.75 per Rs 100. This BTT yields a total of Rs 21.65 Lakh crore using FY 2018-19 RBI payment system data, which is far in excess of the direct and indirect tax collection (in FY 2018-19) of Rs 11.37 lakh crore and Rs 9.39 lakh crore respectively. This coupled with a fact that a flat GST of 5% is also being levied should provide enough surplus and cushion to offset and absorb any potential reduction in stamp duty and registration fees collection that may arise due to reduction of stamp duties and registration fees.

Coupled with the earlier measures for direct taxes especially, the above will help eliminate the single largest source of black money in India.

Overall, the importance of the real estate sector in kick-starting the Indian economy cannot be stressed upon enough. There are allied industries like construction, cement, steel and others that feed into the real estate sector. Increased activity in all of these industries would contribute to the sector's growth and thereby enhance its contribution to overall employment and income generation.

Overall, if the suggested reforms in this chapter are carried out in the interim and corruption eliminated from the process of acquiring licenses and approval of real estate project permits, and if compliance with safety standards and other requisites are ensured, the realty sector might be able to survive the drying up of the lubricant that kept it well-oiled and find ways to reinvent itself without losing its inherent strengths.

Without a doubt, a vibrant real estate sector should help to (re)create millions of jobs and thereby bolster the growth of the Indian economy. If the Indian economy is to grow at rates greater than 15 percent, then, undoubtedly, reforms in the real estate sector would have to play a huge role in the economic reforms process.

Coupled with the earlier measures, the above will help eliminate the single largest source of black money in India.

3A. Restructure anti-corruption bodies like the Lokpal and Lokayuktas to root out corruption and the associated parallel (black) economy

The monitoring of corruption and action against people who indulge in it (especially those holding public office) must be top notch and fool proof. The Lokpal and Lokayuktas must have clear cut transparent norms for appointment of their members (with adequate representation for gender, etc.) as well as the (executive) powers to be exercised. Members of Lokpal and Lokayuktas must have the highest level of integrity and competence and must not have any political affiliation. Their qualifications and functions must be precisely and transparently operationalized. More details about this are given in chapter 3, which is exclusively devoted to fighting corruption on a national basis. This is a very necessary step required to eliminate corruption at various levels of the government, which is the bane of modern Indian society. The following are the strategic recommendations in this regard:

a) Lokpal and Lokayuktas must be truly independent bodies without any conflicts of interest so that they can be the effective tool to fight corruption of all kinds—regular as well as spectacular corruption.

b) For this, the first requirement is to make the Lokpal and Lokayuktas appropriate in terms of member composition without any conflicts of interest (CoI). Furthermore, members should have impeccable credentials and highest levels of professional and personal integrity. This would encompass taking care of political, private sector, civil service and government related conflicts of interest. This in turn requires a CoI subset of rules to be a part of the Lokpal and Lokayuktas legislation and members must be mandatorily required to provide a CoI self-declaration. Furthermore, the composition of Lokpal and Lokayuktas must be decided by a broad based committee comprising heads of governments, leaders of opposition and chief justices of Supreme and High Courts' along with significant participation by eminent people from civil society.

c) The Lokpal and Lokayuktas must have the jurisdiction to enquire and provide punishment to all involved in regular and spectacular corruption. The term all would include politicians and civil servants, of all kinds and grades, the judiciary, constitutional and government functionaries (including Prime Minister, Chief Ministers and Ministers) and all others holding elected office including MPs and MLAs, right from the President of India to the *sarpanch* of the smallest revenue village at the local level. Additionally, all officials serving at various levels of government and in varying capacities and belonging to different categories must also come under the Lokpal and Lokayuktas, as per jurisdiction.

d) An independent body without CoI must be set up to investigate the corruption cases that get referred to and come under the jurisdiction of the Lokpal and the Lokayuktas.

e) The body must be a national level institution comprising of a broad based civil society dominant, politically neutral board. It must have a headquarters office in Delhi as well as offices in all the states. All of these offices would come under the purview of the Right to Information (RTI) act.

f) The best and most efficient, yet patriotic officers with impeccable integrity from the IPS must occupy leadership positions in such a body. The organization must also have officers of impeccable integrity, efficiency and patriotism from the Internal Revenue Service (IRS), Indian Administrative Service (IAS), Indian Foreign Service (IFS) and other services as appropriate.

g) The officers of the independent investigative organization must have all the necessary executive powers required for the investigation and solving of corruption cases. The organization's officers must report through a proper chain of command to the senior management and CEO of the institution who in turn would apprise the board. The board will forward the extant recommendations to the respective Lokpal and/or Lokayuktas for action.

h) All officers and people involved with the Lokpal and the Lokayuktas will have to declare all assets - (income, shares, jewellery etc) and file annual returns as specified in the recommendation on tax reforms given in chapter 1. The compensation provided to all the staff of this entire Lokpal and Lokayuktas setup must be in line with the best in country so that they can discharge their roles and duties without fear, favor and prejudice and in the most efficient and effective manner.

3B. Bringing radical change in the governance of government and its institutions to eliminate corruption, enhance effectiveness and efficiency in their working and facilitate accountability in real time is a very necessary corollary as well and the Lokpal and Lokayuktas must enable this.

a) Governance of government and its institutions needs radical change. Over the last 72 years, in many instances, corruption has been rampant and arrogance has been high among those politicians holding office as well as government officials. Of course, there are several exceptions to this but across the board, the above is true and representative of many governments in India. Things have however started to change in recent times but a lot more needs to be done. Without a doubt, governments need to move to community sensitive governance and become more efficient (do things the right way), effective (do the right things) and adaptive (innovate and adapt in real time to the situation). Lokpal and the Lokayuktas must facilitate this through their regular body of work.

b) Corruption, by and large, has been rampant at all levels of government over the last 72 years because of which the prices of goods and services in the country increases consistently. Money making has become more the norm rather than the exception, especially for a government official. From getting a village officer's certificate to clearances for larger industries and/or contracts for supply of goods and services to the government, money needs to be paid out (by and large). This has to change completely and accountability must come into the system. Again, the Lokpal and the Lokayuktas must facilitate this.

c) Implementation of schemes is also poor and very little reaches the common man relative to the expenditure. Regular as well as spectacular corruption including use of middlemen for the same are key issues here and this again needs the close attention of Lokpal and Lokayuktas.

d) Middlemen have been ruling the roost for over 72 years now and as a result, the transactions cost and also (wasteful) government expenditure increases. A large amount of corruption takes place due to the presence of middlemen and the Lokpal and Lokayuktas must help tackle this menace and put an end to it, once and for all by showcasing examples of such corruption and punishing the people concerned in a serious and stringent manner.

e) While good officials exist at all levels, they are far and few relative to the corrupt group and where they resist, they are penalized. This aspect also needs attention of the Lokpal and Lokayuktas.

f) Thus, the Lokpal and Lokayuktas and their infrastructure must be strengthened to check corruption, ensure accountability and enhance efficiency and effectiveness in the delivery of government services. While an assault on corruption can achieve this, much of what is stated above needs to be closely monitored by the Lokpal/ Lokayuktas.

g) This apart, several other issues must be factored in by the Lokpal/Lokayuktas:

- ☞ Reducing unnecessary government expenditure is absolutely necessary to have a better economy and every department must use process mapping and value engineering to eliminate redundancy in paperwork and processes so as to reduce wasteful government activities and associated expenditure. When this is achieved, corruption will automatically come down.
- ☞ The utility of the government schemes must be continuously evaluated by an independent broad based pan India body like the CAG, which must be made completely independent of government control. It goes without saying that the appointment process of the CAG must be made totally independent of the ruling dispensation just as in the case of the

Lokpal/Lokayuktas. The recommendations so made by the CAG with regard to schemes must be implemented immediately and schemes deemed to be useless to the people must be scrapped in totality.

- In fact, the government must encourage entrepreneurship and move towards "minimum government and maximum governance". All unnecessary licensing and approval requirements must be streamlined to reduce government footprint in all wakes of life. This will bring down corruption significantly.
- A special grievances handling mechanism that automatically and independently reaches the Lokpal structure for corruption related matters and a similar one that reaches the Comptroller and Auditor General (CAG) for efficiency and effectiveness of services must be established immediately.
- All elected representatives occupying government office, elected representatives and government officials at all levels must come under the conflict of interest sub-rules as per the Lokpal and Lokayukta structures. Several declarations will have to be made by them while assuming office and subsequently on an annual basis. This will prevent corruption in a big way.

All of the above should reduce wasteful government expenditure and enhance efficiency and effectiveness of governance while simultaneously eliminating corruption and reducing the footprint of governments in various sectors in line with the motto, "minimum government, maximum governance".

4. Reform public procurement and sourcing of services/materials for government/public use in India through the enactment and implementation of a public procurement act

A special act must be created and passed with regard to the governance of public procurement. Among other things, this act will lay down specifics to be accomplished while going in for tendering of natural resources, procuring defense equipment and so on including reservation of procurement for MSMEs by gender, etc. See chapter 4 for further details. It needs to be noted that all developed countries have a strong public procurement act and India is one of the few with a weak public procurement system. This is a very necessary and crucial aspect that needs urgent attention. Accordingly, the following steps are suggested:

a) The Government of India must immediately pass a public procurement and services/materials sourcing act in India as public procurement and services/material sourcing has been and can be a major source of corruption. The same has to be accepted by all state legislatures and implemented in real time by the government of India and state governments.

b) The act must be comprehensive and cover extraction and sale of all natural resources (raw materials, minerals, intangible assets like spectrum, etc.) in India, whether at the central or state or local government level. The same act must also be the basis for sourcing of goods and services by the government for public use—be it in infrastructure or other sectors.

c) The act must ensure complete transparency and accountability in the public procurement and services/materials sourcing processes, so that revenue from national resources and needs are at least optimized, if not maximized.

d) All public procurement must come under the audit and inspection of the Comptroller and Auditor General of India (CAG). All constitutional bodies {including the Reserve Bank of India (RBI)} as well as government and/or government aided institutions must come under a CAG audit with regards to public procurement and sourcing of services/materials for their own and public use.

e) It goes without saying that the appointment of the CAG must be streamlined and free of political and other biases and conflicts of interest. The CAG must be completely independent of the government so that an impartial, objective and candid assessment of the public procurement and goods/services sourcing processes in the entire country is possible in real time.

Thus, eliminating corruption in public procurement and goods/services sourcing is very central to building a robust economy and the above are the most urgent tasks that need to be undertaken immediately (in conjunction with other recommendations made in this book), especially, if we desire India to witness double digit growth in the near future.

5. Re-engineer the political system to eliminate corruption and have a vibrant democracy so vital for a strong, resilient economy

The aspect of political funding must be streamlined and all political parties should not be allowed to accept cash donations of more than Rs 500. All political parties must come under the RTI Act. Furthermore, no person can be an elected representative in the same position for more than 2 terms. Comprehensive details on the political reform required are provided below:

a) First concerns the political processes. Much of the malaise that arises from the political economy is the lack of alternatives. The first step required is for the political system to create choices. That can only be done by limiting the number of terms for any person in an elected position to a maximum of two terms, irrespective of the political office. This will go a long way in promoting choice, reducing dependence on personality oriented politics and eliminating corruption. There can, however, be no restrictions on party positions. Also, candidates with proven criminal records and convictions cannot contest elections. Those with ongoing criminal cases (that are neither politically motivated nor fall under activist demonstration cases) cannot contest until their cases are over and/or a no objection is provided by the competent court.

b) Every election requires a candidate to spend money and this is the root cause of corruption. This needs serious reforms. What is proposed is as follows:

   i. State funding of elections where by a Lok Sabha Member of Parliament (MP) will get Rs 5 crore, Rajya Sabha MP will get Rs 50 lakh, an MLA will get Rs 2 crore and so on as may be decided by the election commission in consultation with the key stakeholders. A total of Rs 50000 crore can be spent on election expenditure per election cycle. Candidates who met certain criteria alone (to be framed by the CEC after a nationwide consultation) will be eligible for state election funds. Those who receive state election funds must submit daily expenses to the central election commission (CEC) with a one-week time lag at maximum.

   ii. Candidates will be allowed to form Political Action Committees (PACs), which can collect and spend money for and on behalf of political parties and candidates. PACs will have to be body corporates and can function nationally, state wise and at local level. They have to be registered with the central election commission (CEC) and follow forms norms and rules of the CEC which would include daily reporting of their expenditure to the

CEC, with a maximum time lag of seven days. PACs will have restrictions on the amount they can spend per candidate. PACs will be subject to strict CAG AUDIT and also CEC audits to prevent diversion of money—e.g., bribing of voters which is an aspect that has become very common in India, especially during the last decade. PACs WILL also have to file annual returns. All monies received by PACs will be subject to a 25 percent election tax at the receiver's end which will go into the CECs pool of funds. It is believed that the above would play a huge role in enabling state funding of elections. Coupled with the earlier measures on taxation and other reforms regarding corruption, state funding of elections should enhance transparency and accountability in the electoral system.

c) Apart from b i) and ii) above, candidates cannot spend any money on elections.

d) All monies contributed over Rs 500 will have to be paid digitally.

e) Candidates will not be allowed to bribe or pay voters for their votes. Anyone caught doing this or contravening any of the above norms will be debarred from contesting any election for life. Additionally, severe punishments in terms of life sentences of up to 10 years may also be considered as bribing of voters is a very serious offence.

It is believed that if the above reforms are carried out, corruption, which is the bane of Indian politics, will disappear and we can have a healthy democracy contributing to a healthy economy as well, which can grow at double digit rates, provide greater employment and reduce poverty and inequality as well.

Lastly, even while I have discussed the need to bridge the digital divide briefly in an earlier chapter, I would like to sign off by re-emphasizing on issues related to the switch to the digital economy, given its positioning as the optimal way forward.

First off is the need for an ecosystem that supports the transition to the digital space in a smooth manner. Data connectivity continues to be a challenge in many parts of the country, despite the reported upgrade from 3G to 4G. In the absence of access to the internet, most mobile applications (apps) would be rendered useless. It is critical to ensure data connectivity in every nook and corner of the country, but, equally important is the need to provide backup services in the event of the lack of network access.

Again, continued availability of electricity is also a critical factor. That our systems are not hardy enough to withstand the vagaries of the weather is proven by Chennai's experiences during Cyclone Vardah in December 2016. Even as the city suffered from a lack of access to electricity, data connectivity and even mobile networks, the digital ecosystem completely collapsed, leaving the city's population without any means of transacting, given the already prevalent cash crunch.

Process and digital literacy is yet another critical need right now. Before we push people headlong into the digital stream, it would be useful if we at least imparted basic survival skills needed to negotiate the new waters and stay afloat. The digital instruments that currently populate the market are designed for those with a fair degree of understanding of both the financial and the digital process. The population that still remains excluded from the formal financial process, and which the country hopes to bring into the digital fold, is not highly literate, both in terms of the process as well as familiarity with the digital space.

There is also the constraint imposed by language. Even if vernacular options are available, the complex language and syntax puts them above the reach of a semi-literate population. Then there is the challenge involved with comprehending the financial transaction process and negotiating its various steps. Clearly, there is a need for process and digital literacy tools and aids, without which it is going to be very difficult for low-income people to use digital finance options. Actual use of these digital finance mechanisms (DFMs) have to be facilitated through applications that handhold the customer and promote digital and process literacy of the end-user in real time, thereby bolstering the use of DFMs.

There are also anti-trust implications that need to be considered in the present scenario. While there are a plethora of players in the digital financial space, there is also scope for monopoly by resorting to unfair trade practises, undercutting opponents and so on. The practice of using capital revenues to fund such practices in the form of cash-backs, for example, is not a healthy trend. One must draw a parallel with the situation in the call taxi space in India, where Ola and Uber have more or less driven out the competition by offering superior service at par or even below par prices. The danger is that once they have consolidated their market shares sufficiently, they may jack up prices and the loyal client-base would be forced to continue their patronage, in the absence of viable alternatives. It is important that we guard against the emergence of such a situation in the digital financial services space.

Also important are the unique risks that the digital economy faces, which needs safeguarding against. Unfortunately, no such safeguards exist currently, to the best of my knowledge.[211] These risks are both known and unknown. Known risks pertain to the safety of digital money, and the experience of Venezuela is a strong case in point. Unknown risks include natural and man-made calamities like the Cyclone Vardah experience referred to earlier. Although it underlined the lack of robustness in our infrastructural systems, it also caught the citizens unaware and resulted in a significant period of hardship when they had no means of making

---

[211] See 'Venezuela warns about cybercrime', December 13, 2016, *The Hindu,* Kallol Bhattacherjee,
http://www.thehindu.com/news/national/Venezuela-warns-about-cybercrime/article16801504.ece

transactions.[212] The Manipur[213] situation is another case in point where the administration had blocked data access with a view to containing riot like situations. Likewise, the practical issues associated with blocking of internet in other regions (such as Kashmir in August 2019 or the north eastern India in December 2019) to ensure law and order need to be considered. Therefore, it is clear that all possible risks associated with the transition to a digital ecosystem need to be thoroughly considered and tackled through an appropriate framework. I would strongly recommend an urgent **yet comprehensive digital ecosystem risk audit**, by an independent agency with no commercial interests in the digital space. The need for an independent third party agency is to avoid conflicts of interests.

In addition, to take care of cybercrime, specialized task forces with qualified people on board—at district and state levels—need to be established. This is to ensure the speedy resolution of criminal cases, especially where consumers have been the victims of cybercrime.

A related issue here is the privacy of data—without a doubt, the digital footprint should not be the cause for creating a security risk for individuals and/or

---

[212] See 'No Cash, No Card. How Cyclone Vardah Has Crippled Chennai's Cashless Drive', December 15, 2016, *NDTV*, J Sam Daniel Stalin, http://www.ndtv.com/chennai-news/no-cash-no-card-how-cyclone-vardah-has-crippled-chennais-cashless-drive-1637991
[213] See 'Manipur Govt extends suspension of mobile data for another week', December 27, 2016, *The Indian Express*, ANI http://indianexpress.com/article/india/manipur-govt-extends-suspension-of-mobile-data-for-another-week-4446726/

result in the misuse of their personal data. For example, mobile wallets[214] ask for access to a variety of personal data at the time of installation, so much of which do not even appear relevant to their purpose. Also, there is no transparency in terms of the exact data being accessed or used, which the consumer is entitled to know. A privacy act with sufficient teeth must, therefore, be enacted immediately to safeguard the data of consumers who leave a digital footprint.

It would serve the transition well in this context, if a Digital Services Consumer Protection Agency (DSCPA) were to be established, on the lines of FINRA[215] (Financial Industry Regulatory Authority), which was established in the United States post the 2008 financial crisis and which has done significant work. The agency could first function as a separate cell under the RBI to look at the above issues and consumer protection aspects in the digital space with a financial exposure, including e-commerce. At a later date, it could be spun off as an independent body with statutory powers.

As part of this, it would also help to have a 24 hour dedicated helpline[216] to redress grievances arising out

---

[214] See 'Your digital wallet can be a 'pickpocket'', December 05, 2016, *The Hindu,* Samarth Bansal,
http://www.thehindu.com/news/national/Your-digital-wallet-can-be-a-%E2%80%98pickpocket%E2%80%99/article16760772.ece
[215] See http://www.finra.org/
[216] The Government of India's policy think tank, NITI Aayog, along with the *National Association of Software and Services Companies* (NASSCOM, a trade association of Indian Information Technology (IT) and Business Process Outsourcing (BPO) industry

of digital financial transactions, again, including e-commerce companies. If complaints are not redressed within a maximum period of 24 hours with regard to any refund[217] to be made to the customer's account, Section 420 under the Indian Penal Code (IPC) should apply to such misdemeanors or oversights on the part of the digital service providers. The DSCPA should also initiate appropriate action separately with regard to such happenings, especially in the case of refunds.

Finally, it is important that digital service providers (both financial and e-commerce) are subjected to independent periodic audits and are rated in terms of their security measures to protect customer privacy and data. Independent specialized rating agencies may be created, like CRISIL[218] for finance companies and M-CRIL[219] for microfinance institutions, to rate the various risks inherent in the services provided by the Digital Service Providers (DSPs) and their ability

---

and the telecom operators has set up a helpline—14444—to address all queries related to digital payments. See 'Dedicated helpline being set up for digital payments', December 29, 2016, *The Indian Express*, IANS, http://indianexpress.com/article/technology/tech-news-technology/dedicated-helpline-being-set-up-for-digital-payments-4449873/—This is in contrast to the helpline mentioned above—in the text—which is envisaged more as a statutory helpline that can help address consumer grievances.

[217] In some cases, the credit/debit card gets debited but the service is not activated. A classic example is the top up recharge of prepaid mobiles. The refund process normally takes between two to four days (and sometimes even longer), which is unfair as the customer neither has the service nor gets the money back {which is still retained by the digital finance service provider or telecommunications company (TELCO) for a few/several days}.

[218] See http://www.crisil.com/index.jsp

[219] See http://www.m-cril.com/

167

to mitigate those, especially from the perspective of protecting customer privacy and data. Such ratings should also provide insight into the ability of the DSP's to manage newer and newer risks occurring in the digital ecosystem, given that technology is often leapfrogged.

Well begun is half done, they say. It is important that due weight is given to all these concerns and the digital ecosystem is empowered upfront to deal with any anomalies that may arise while going forward. Permanent solutions need to found rather than quick fix solutions to any lacunae that may be identified.

The country has been through testing times. Even in the face of adversity, the people have stoically borne inconveniences/losses in the hope of a corruption free economy that will yield benefit to all. There is no denying the benefits that the country would gain from the transition to a less-cash economy, especially in the medium and long term. Hopefully, the government will come up with all the back-up measures needed to tackle the issue of corruption and black money generation and provide the springboard that will not only catapult the economy back on to its feet but also help build a robust digital ecosystem to enable a smooth transition from a 'cash economy' to a 'less-cash economy'.[220]

---

[220] See 'No economy can be fully cashless, it can be 'less cash': Jaitley', December 16, 2016, *The Pioneer,*
http://www.dailypioneer.com/todays-newspaper/no-economy-can-be--fully-cashless-it-can--be-less-cash-jaitley.html

Once the above recommendations are carried out, it is expected that the various pillars of economic growth will automatically start to move and move at a faster pace. Ultimately, the above should enhance domestic consumption and savings, turbo charge exports and also provide for rationalized government expenditure (through a minimum government, maximum transparent governance) without burdening the common man. Furthermore, the current size of the economy will be naturally expanded in real terms as all sources of black money would have been plugged and the power of entrepreneurship unleashed to power India towards double digit growth that can mitigate poverty and enhance quality of life for all citizens and put money in their pocket.

In fact, poverty in India cannot be eliminated until and unless GDP growth exceeds double digits. Otherwise, we will be doing mere lip service to the millions who are hugely vulnerable to falling into the poverty trap. Also, India's has a crucial contribution to make to the goal of eliminating global poverty by 2030 as per UN SDG # 1.

In summary, India has tried everything and it is time to embrace practical economics (with minimum government, maximum governance) to unleash entrepreneurship and power India to double digit growth.

To reiterate, the abolition of personal income tax and corporate tax should put more money in the pocket of the common man and help increase domestic consumption and savings. Together, the abolition of direct taxes and the rationalization of GST should help in building a more competitive industrial base in India, especially among MSMEs and also in manufacturing in general. Various manufacturing clusters that are doing badly should now be able to do better and without a doubt, exports will pick up. The introduction of the BTT coupled with the 5 percent GST should provide enough surplus for government investment in the much needed infrastructure.

The steps for monitoring and action against corruption, the enactment of a public procurement act and the reforms in the realty sector will help immensely in reducing the black money component in the economy as will the aspect of political and electoral reform. These will also root out crony capitalism, which has been the bane of the Indian economy.

Taken together, all of these steps should help create a vibrant and dynamic economy rooted in a sound political ecosystem. That is what India needs today and that is what will cure our ailing age old system of economic governance and push us into an era of dynamic and vibrant entrepreneurship based on sound fundamentals into a period of long lasting double digit growth.

Appendix 1

Contribution of Direct Taxes to Total Tax Revenue

Contribution Of Direct Taxes to Total Tax Revenue				
Financial Year	Direct Taxes (Rs. crore)	Indirect Taxes (Rs. crore)	Total Taxes (Rs. crore)	Direct Tax As % Of Total Taxes
2000-01	68,305	1,19,814	1,88,119	36.31%
2001-02	69,198	1,17,318	1,86,516	37.10%
2002-03	83,088	1,32,608	2,15,696	38.52%
2003-04	1,05,088	1,48,608	2,53,696	41.42%
2004-05	1,32,771	1,70,936	3,03,707	43.72%
2005-06	1,65,216	1,99,348	3,64,564	45.32%
2006-07	2,30,181	2,41,538	4,71,719	48.80%
2007-08	3,14,330	2,79,031	5,93,361	52.97%
2008-09	3,33,818	2,69,433	6,03,251	55.34%
2009-10	3,78,063	2,43,939	6,22,002	60.78%
2010-11	4,45,995	3,43,716	7,89,711	56.48%
2011-12	4,93,987	3,90,953	8,84,940	55.82%
2012-13	5,58,989	4,72,915	10,31,904	54.17%
2013-14	6,38,596	4,95,347	11,33,943	56.32%
2014-15	6,95,792	5,43,215	12,39,007	56.16%
2015-16	7,41,945	7,11,885	14,54,180	51.03%
2016-17	8,49,713	8,61,515	17,11,228	49.65%
2017-18	10,02,037	9,15,256	19,18,210	52.24%
2018-19*	11,37,685	9,39,018	20,76,703	54.78%

* Provisional
Source: 'Income Tax Department Time Series Data Financial Year 2000-01 to 2018-19', Issued by Central Board Of Direct Taxes, https://www.incometaxindia.gov.in/Documents/Direct%20Tax%20Data/IT-Department-Time-Series-Data-FY-2000-01-to-2018-19.pdf

Appendix 1A

Payment System Indicators – Annual Turnover

Payment System Indicators – Annual Turnover						
Item	Volume (million)			Value (Rs billion)		
	2016-17	2017-18	2018-19	2016-17	2017-18	2018-19
1	2	3	4	5	6	7
Systemically Important Financial Market Infrastructures (SIFMIs)						
1. RTGS	107.8	124.4	136.6	981,904	1,167,125	1,356,882
Total Financial Markets Clearing (2 to 4)	3.7	3.5	3.6	1,056,173	1,074,802	1,165,510
2. CBLO	0.2	0.2	0.1	229,528	283,308	181,405
3. Government Securities Clearing	1.5	1.1	1.1	404,389	370,364	509,316
4. Forex Clearing	1.9	2.2	2.4	422,256	421,131	474,790
Total SIFMIs (1 to 4)	**111.5**	**127.9**	**140.2**	**2,038,077**	**2,241,927**	**2,522,392**
Retail Payments						
Total Paper Clearing (5+6)	1,206.7	1,170.6	1,123.8	80,958	81,893	82,461
5. CTS	1,111.9	1,138.00	1,111.7	74,035	79,451	81,536
6. Non-MICR Clearing	94.8	32.6	12.1	6,923	2,442	925
Total Retail Electronic Clearing (7 to 12)	4,222.9	6,382.3	12,466.7	132,324	193,113	267,515
7. ECS DR	8.8	1.5	0.9	39	10	12.6
8. ECS CR	10.1	6.1	5.4	144	115	132.35
9. NEFT	1,622.1	1,946.4	2,318.9	120,040	172,229	227,936
10. IMPS	506.7	1,009.8	1,752.9	4,116	8,925	15,903
11 UPI	17.9	915.2	5,353.4	69	1,098	8,770
12. NACH	2,057.3	2,503.3	3,035.2	7,916	10,736	14,762
Total Card	**5,450.1**	**8,207.6**	**10,781.2**	**7,421**	**10,607**	**14,097**

| Payment System Indicators – Annual Turnover |||||||
| Item | Volume (million) ||| Value (Rs billion) |||
	2016-17	2017-18	2018-19	2016-17	2017-18	2018-19
1	2	3	4	5	6	7
Payments (13 to 15)						
13. Credit Cards	1,087.1	1,405.2	1,762.6	3,284	4,590	6,033
14. Debit Cards	2,399.3	3,343.4	4,414.3	3,299	4,601	5,935
15. PPIs	1,963.7	3,459.0	4,604.3	838	1,416	2,129
Total Retail Payments (5 to 15)	10,879.7	15,760.5	24,371.6	220,703	285,613	364,073
Grand Total (1 to 15)	10,991.2	15,888.4	24,511.9	2,258,780	2,527,540	2,886,465

Notes: 1. RTGS system includes customer and inter-bank transactions only.
2. Settlement of CBLO, government securities clearing and forex transactions is through the Clearing Corporation of India Ltd. (CCIL). Government Securities include outright trades and both legs of repo transactions and Tri-party repo transactions.
3. CCIL discontinued operations of CBLO from November 5, 2018. Tri-party Repo under Securities segment was operationalized by CCIL on November 5, 2018.
4. The figures for cards are for transactions at point of sale (POS) terminals only which include online transactions.
5. Figures in the columns might not add up to the total due to rounding off of numbers.

Source: 'Annual Report 2018-2019', RBI, https://m.rbi.org.in/Scripts/AnnualReportPublications.aspx?Id=1264

Appendix 1B[1]

Economic Growth Articles for India

1. Amadeo, Kimberly, 'India's Economy, Its Challenges, Opportunities, and Impact', July 03, 2019, https://www.thebalance.com/india-s-economy-3306348
2. Basu, Kaushik, 'India and the Mistrust Economy', November 6, 2019, https://www.nytimes.com/2019/11/06/opinion/india-economy.html
3. Chakravarty, Praveen, 'Viewpoint: How serious is India's economic slowdown?', August 27, 2019, https://www.bbc.com/news/world-asia-india-49470466
4. Choudhary, Shrimi, 'Karvy fiasco: How brokers exploited the loopholes', December 09, 2019, Business Standard, Rediff, https://www.rediff.com/business/report/karvy-fiasco-how-brokers-exploited-the-loopholes/20191209.htm
5. Das, Koustav, 'Make or break: Why next 2 months will be crucial for Indian economy', September 4, 2019, *India Today,* https://www.indiatoday.in/news-analysis/story/indian-economy-slowdown-revival-measures-next-two-months-crucial-1595216-2019-09-04
6. India Today Web Desk, 'Gross Domestic Product growth falls to 4.5% in Q2 of 2019-20', November 29, 2019, https://www.indiatoday.in/business/story/gross-domestic-product-growth-falls-4-5-per-cent-q2-2019-20-1623733-2019-11-29
7. Kapoor, Amit, 'The dynamics of India's growth slowdown', September 09, 2019, IANS, https://economictimes.indiatimes.com/news/economy/indicators/the-dynamics-of-indias-growth-recession/articleshow/71020942.cms?from=mdr
8. Kriplani, Jash, 'Equity flows see sharpest dip in 3.5 years, slip 78% in November', December 10, 2019, Business Standard, Rediff, https://www.rediff.com/business/report/equity-flows-see-sharpest-drop-slip-78-in-nov/20191210.htm

---

[1] Compiled from data found in various documents of Government of India and other web resources.

9. Livemint.com, 'Fundamentals of Indian economy continue to be strong; Q3 GDP may pick up: CEA', November 29, 2019, https://www.livemint.com/news/india/fundamentals-of-indian-economy-continue-to-be-strong-q3-gdp-may-pick-up-cea-11575038409083.html
10. Moss, Daniel, 'View: With growth this bad, India needs more than luck', November 30, 2019, Bloomberg, https://economictimes.indiatimes.com/news/economy/policy/with-growth-this-bad-india-needs-more-than-luck/articleshow/72302855.cms
11. Ninan, T N, 'Nirmalaji, don't waste this chance!', December 10, 2019, Business Standard, Rediff, https://www.rediff.com/money/column/nirmalaji-dont-waste-this-chance/20191210.htm
12. Paliath, Shreehari, 'The muddle Modi madeNarendra Modi is damaging India's economy as well as its democracy', November 3, 2019, https://www.indiaspend.com/there-are-very-strong-concerns-about-the-indian-economy/
13. Pal, Deepali, '8 Major Problems Faced by the Indian Economy', http://www.economicsdiscussion.net/indian-economy/problems-indian-economy/8-major-problems-faced-by-the-indian-economy/14140
14. Press Trust of India, 'ADB cuts India's FY19 growth forecast to 5.1%', December 11, 2019, https://www.rediff.com/business/report/adb-cuts-indias-fy19-growth-forecast-to-51/20191211.htm
15. Press Trust of India, 'Car sales dip marginally in November', December 10, 2019, https://www.rediff.com/business/report/auto-car-sales-dip-marginally-in-november/20191210.htm
16. Press Trust of India, 'Voda Idea will shut down without govt relief: Birla', December 06, 2019, Rediff, https://www.rediff.com/business/report/voda-idea-will-shut-down-without-govt-relief-birla/20191206.htm
17. Press Trust of India, 'More bad news, Goldman pegs FY20 GDP growth at 5.3%', December 03, 2019, https://www.rediff.com/business/report/more-bad-news-goldman-pegs-fy20-gdp-growth-to-53/20191203.htm
18. Press Trust of India, 'Indian economy currently facing challenges, says Sitharaman', November 10, 2019, https://economictimes.indiatimes.com/news/economy/policy/indian-economy-currently-facing-challenges-says-sitharaman/articleshow/71996526.cms?from=mdr

19. Rediff.com, 'Crisil sharply cuts FY20 growth forecast to 5.1%', December 02, 2019, https://www.rediff.com/business/report/crisil-sharply-cuts-fy20-growth-forecast-to-51/20191202.htm
20. Rediff.com, 'GDP is expected to pick up in Q3, says CEA Subramanian', November 29, 2019, https://www.rediff.com/business/report/gdp-is-expected-to-pick-up-in-q3-says-cea-subramanian/20191129.htm
21. Rediff.com, 'GDP growth sputters to 4.5%, weakest in over 6 years', November 29, 2019, https://m.rediff.com/money/report/crisis-deepens-q2-gdp-growth-slips-to-45/20191129.htm
22. Rediff.com, 'Core sector output shrinks by 5.8% in October', November 29, 2019, https://www.rediff.com/business/report/core-sector-output-shrinks-by-58-in-october/20191129.htm
23. Toppr, 'Development Issues of Indian Economy', https://www.toppr.com/guides/business-economics-cs/overview-of-indian-economy/development-issues-of-indian-economy/
24. Vyas, Mahesh 'Beware! Economy headed for greater trouble', December 13, 2019, Business Standard, Rediff, https://www.rediff.com/business/column/beware-economy-headed-for-greater-trouble/20191213.htm
25. Vita, Stephen, '3 Economic Challenges for India in 2019', May 24, 2019, Investopedia, https://www.investopedia.com/articles/investing/012516/3-economic-challenges-india-faces-2016.asp
26. Warrier, Shobha 'India becoming 3rd largest economy is not far away', December 04, 2019, https://www.rediff.com/business/interview/india-becoming-3rd-largest-economy-is-not-far-away/20191204.htm
27. Waghmare, Abhishek, 'Explained in Charts: Indian economy loses sheen', December 03, 2019, Business Standard, https://www.rediff.com/business/report/explained-in-charts-indian-economy-loses-sheen/20191203.htm

Appendix 1C

Digital Solutions

With a view to enabling users to cross barriers imposed by literacy and language and make better use of digital technology to conduct financial transactions, I propose the following products primarily designed to benefit the poor, the rural population and those who continue to remain excluded from the formal financial system.

The first solution is a voice led mobile application that will help users negotiate mobile payment gateways and mobile banking systems, undaunted by language, digital and process literacy. The sections of the population that still remain excluded from the digital financial systems are handicapped by a lack of comprehension of the processes and their working. They need to be imparted digital and process literacy before they can effectively use the available solutions. Yet, given the situation at hand, these users need to be brought up to speed in a hurry. Hence training and educating the users can, at best, be a parallel process and they need to be enabled to get on the digital bandwagon straight up.

It is with a view to making this possible that I propose a voice led mobile app that will hand hold the user through the transaction process. The user will be guided through the various options and screens in the simplest and friendliest manner and the 'virtual voice' will be with him[2] every step of the way, telling him what to do. The mobile app will be location specific and therefore it will choose to speak to the user in the language of the region that he lives in. The option of changing the language to one of his choice will also be afforded to him. Starting with basic financial transactions like sending and receiving money, the app will be upgraded to enable the use of more complex functions like bill payments, purchase of train/bus/flight tickets, and even using e-commerce sites.

---

[2] Him is used without bias to refer to any person—male/female/other

The Prepaid Debit Cards

Although prepaid debit cards exist in the market from banks such as SBI, IDBI and HDFC, the proposed solution intends to follow the prepaid SIM card model in terms of acquisition and top up of the card balance. It can use the strength of the microfinance sector for its distribution with a techno start-up offering back-end solutions.

The prepaid card can be co-branded by the techno start-up with a nationalized bank and can be made available through the network of microfinance institutions and their field workers. Made available for a minimal entry free, the customer can subsequently keep adding balance to his prepaid card through the deposit of money with the field workers of the microfinance institutions. These field workers will pass on information on the top-up required digitally to the start-up, which will then convey the credit to the cardholder in collaboration with the bank. Appropriate internal control mechanisms will have to be in place during the implementation of this solution. The techno start-up may hold a certain fixed balance with the bank, which can be debited every time the credit needs to be conveyed to the cardholder. The field workers will deposit the cash with the microfinance institutions, which will, in turn, convey the credit to the techno start-up. The cardholders can use the cards at all outlets that accept Visa/Master/RuPay cards and can also withdraw money from ATMs across the country. The techno start-up can be a collaborative venture between the providers of the digital back end solutions, who also undertake distribution responsibilities of the cards, the banks and the microfinance network. The cards can be used to issue loans to MSMEs through the SHG network and under the Cooperative/Grameen/MFI model, and also for loan installment collection by the field workers under various options.

Appendix 1D

State-wise Stamp Duty and Registration Fees in India

States	Criteria	Stamp Duty	Registration Fees
Andhra Pradesh	Sale Deed	5%	0.50%
	Conveyance Deed (gift, mortgage, lease etc.)	5%	0.50% (Subject to a minimum of Rs.1000/- and maximum of Rs.10,000/-)
	Agreement of Sale cum General Power of Attorney	6%	Rs. 2000/-
	Development Agreement cum General Power of Attorney	1%	0.5 (Subject to a maximum of Rs.20,000/-)
Arunachal Pradesh	Sale Deed	6%	
Assam	Sale Deed	8.25%	
Bihar		☞ In case of transfer from male to female 5.7% ☞ In case of transfer from female to male 6.3%, ☞ In any other case 6%.	☞ In case of transfer from male to female 1.9% ☞ In case of transfer from female to male 2.1% ☞ In any other case 2%.
Chhattisgarh	Sale Deed	5%	-
Delhi	Sale Deed and Conveyance Deed	Male 6%	1%
		Female 4%	1%
Goa	None	☞ Upto Rs 50	

States	Criteria	Stamp Duty	Registration Fees
		lakh - 3.5% ☞ Rs 50 - Rs 75 lakh - 4% ☞ Rs 75 - Rs 1 crore - 4.5% ☞ Over Rs 1 crore - 5%	
Gujarat	Sale/Conveyance Deed	4.90%	1%
Haryana	Sale Deed	For male - 6% in rural areas and 8% in urban areas For female - 4% in rural areas and 6% in urban areas	
Himachal Pradesh	Sale, Gift and Mortgage with possession	5%	2%
Jharkhand	Sale/Conveyance Deed	4%	3%
	Mortgage	4.2%	2%
Jammu & Kashmir	Sale Deed	5%	
Karnataka	Conveyance (Sale)	5%	1%
Kerala	Conveyance (Sale)	8%	2%
Maharashtra	Within Municipal Corporation boundary	6%	1%
	Within Municipal Council boundary	4%	1%
	Within Gram Panchayat boundary	3%	1%
Madhya Pradesh	None	5%	
Manipur	None	4%	3%
Meghalaya	Sale Deed	9.9%	
Mizoram	Sale Deed	9%	
Nagaland	Sale Deed	8.25%	
Odisha	Sale Deed	Male 5% Female 4%	2%
Punjab	None	6%	1%
Rajasthan	Sale/Conveyance Deed	Male 5% Female 4%	1%
Sikkim	Sale Deed	4% (in case of	3%

\multicolumn{4}{c}{State-wise Stamp Duty and Registration Fees in India}
States	**Criteria**	**Stamp Duty**	**Registration Fees**
		Sikkimese origin) 9% (for others)	
Tamil Nadu	Conveyance (Sale)	7%	4%
	Exchange	7% on the market value of the greater value.	
	Simple Mortgage	1% (on the loan amount) subject to a maximum of Rs.40,000/-	1% on loan amount subject to a maximum of Rs.10,000/-
Telangana	Sale	5%	0.5%
Tripura	Sale	5%	
Uttar Pradesh	Sale Deed	7%	1%
Uttarakhand	Sale Deed	Male - 5% Female - 3.75%	
West Bengal	Within Municipal boundary	6%	1.10%
	Outside Municipal boundary	5%	1.10%
\multicolumn{4}{l}{This has been compiled from various websites and state government information sources.}

Appendix 2A

Published Books, Articles, Papers & Unpublished Reports

Published Books (Not-Exhaustive)

1. Arunachalam Ramesh S (2019), "Central Bank Mandates, Autonomy and Accountability", *SMW*, Chennai. Available worldwide.
2. Arunachalam Ramesh S (2018), "Piercing The Corporate Veil", *SMW*, Chennai. Available worldwide.
3. Arunachalam Ramesh S (2018), "Never Waste A Crisis", *SMW*, Chennai. Available worldwide.
4. Arunachalam Ramesh S (2018), "Powering A Billion Dreams", *SMW*, Chennai. Available worldwide.
5. Arunachalam Ramesh S (2017), "The Cinderella Notes: Demonetization and the Indian Economy", *SMW,* Chennai and *Createspace,* USA. See *reviews* on amazon.in and by Matthew S Gamser at amazon.com. See Prof Malcolm Harper's Review and See Sukhwinder Arora's Review of this book. This is a critically acclaimed and hugely popular book and had 2 chapters devoted to regulation and supervision of commercial banks, NBFCs, Cooperatives etc—in relation to inclusive finance (MSME, agri, micro and other pro-poor/rural financial services)
6. Arunachalam Ramesh S (2015), "Where Angels Prey", *Authors Upfront, Delhi*. See review of this book by Tim Kelley, who called it a modern day version of Pearl S Buck's "Good Earth"— https://forextv.com/top-news/book-review-where-angels-prey-by-ramesh-s-arunachalam/
7. Arunachalam, Ramesh S (2014), "An Idea Which Went Wrong: Commercial Microfinance in India", *SMW*, Chennai and *Createspace,* USA. See review of this book by Milford Bateman at http://microfinance-in-india.blogspot.in/2014/08/milford-batemans-review-of-idea-which.html
8. This again is a critically acclaimed book and held out very important lessons for banking regulation and supervision, financial stability, safety and soundness with regard to commercial bank lending to MSME's, low income people, agriculture and the use of technology based banking. It had 12

chapters dealing with issues related to financial stability, banking regulation and supervision and the like. This books looks at ways in which the governance and accountability as also regulatory and supervisory capacities of central banks can be enhanced.

9. Arunachalam Ramesh S (2011), "The Journey of Indian Micro-Finance: Lessons For the Future" by Aapti Publications, Chennai. See amazon.in and see the review of book by Sucheta Dalal, well known journalist and managing editor Moneylife. This is a critically acclaimed and popular book and it offered very crucial lessons for banking regulation and supervision, financial stability, safety and soundness with regard to commercial bank lending to MSME's, low income people, agriculture and the use of technology based banking. It had 8 chapters dealing with issues related to financial stability, banking regulation and supervision and the like. This book was released by Yezdi Malegam, four time board member of the Reserve Bank of India and the author many of regulatory and supervisory laws and frameworks in India. Malegam is now heading an EXPERT COMMITTEE to look at the banking frauds, NPA situation and banking crisis in India. See review by Milford Bateman

Published/Other Papers (Non-Exhaustive):

1. Arunachalam Ramesh S (2008) "Micro-finance and Innovative Financing for Gender Equality: Approaches, Challenges and Strategies" for 8 WAMM Commonwealth Ministers Meeting", Uganda
2. Arunachalam Ramesh S (2008), "Scoping Paper on Financial Inclusion: Considerations and Recommendations for UNDP", by UNDP India
3. Arunachalam Ramesh S et al (2008) "Enhancing Financial Services Flow to Small Scale Marine Fisheries Sector in India", A Study for FAO/UNTRS
4. Arunachalam Ramesh S (2008) "Micro-Pensions in India: Critical Issues, Challenges and Strategies for Future" Study for MicroNed Network, Netherlands
5. Arunachalam Ramesh S (2009) "Financial Inclusion of Agriculture: Key Challenges and Ways Ahead for Agricultural Finance", Chapter in a Book on Financial and Social Inclusion Edited by Ms Smita Premchander et al, DFID WORLP Project, Orissa
6. Arunachalam Ramesh S et al (2009), "Marketing, Technology and Finance Constraints Related to MSMEs in India: A Status Report of 32 Sectors", Prepared for the National Commission

on Enterprises in the Unorganised Sector (NCEUS), Government of India, New Delhi

7. Arunachalam Ramesh S (2009) "Distribution of Micro-Insurance: Key Challenges and Regulatory Recommendations", Paper published in the Issue of Journal of Insurance, Pravarthak, February 2009.

8. Arunachalam Ramesh S (2008) "UNDP Financial Inclusion Strategy in 7 Focus States: Strategic Consideration and Suggestions", UNDP

9. Arunachalam Ramesh S (2008) "Delivering Vulnerability Reducing Financial Services in an Inclusive Manner: Lessons from Commonwealth Countries for Building A Sustainable and Responsive Microfinance Portfolio", Commonwealth Secretariat and Govt. of Singapore (Paper Presented at Singapore)

10. Arunachalam Ramesh S (2008) "Microfinance and Technology—Critical Issues, Lessons and Future Implications", Paper first written for the Microfinance India *Conference*, Oct 9 – 10th, 2007 New Delhi and subsequently revised significantly and published as part of the CORDAID Research Series, Netherlands

11. Arunachalam Ramesh S et al (2008), "Microfinance and Economic Security: Towards a New Financial Inclusion Paradigm", Paper presented at the *South Asia International Economic Security Conference*, Feb 17–20th, 2008 New Delhi

12. Arunachalam Ramesh S et al (2008), "Urban Poverty, MSMEs, Livelihoods and Microfinance: Critical Issues, Challenges and Strategies for Future", Paper presented at the Urban Poverty *International Conference*, Jan 21st–22nd, 2008, Ahmedabad, India

13. Arunachalam Ramesh S (2008), "Using Technology to Enable Formal Financial Institutions to Deliver Pro-Poor Market Based Financial Services: Areas for Regulatory Reform with Lessons from 4 years of FDCF (DFID) Implementation in India" for Ministry of Finance (MoF), Reserve Bank of India (RBI) and Insurance Regulatory Development Authority (IRDA)

14. Arunachalam, Ramesh S (2009), "The Impact of Financial Crisis on MSMEs and Micro-finance: Strategic Lessons from India, Philippines, Indonesia, Afghanistan, Kenya, Malawi and St Lucia, MCG Paper

15. Arunachalam Ramesh S (2008) "Consolidated Baseline Data on MSME and Financial Service Providers and Institutions in 7 UNDAF States", UNDP

16. Arunachalam Ramesh S (2007) et al, "India Country Scan for Financial Services Design/Delivery to Low Income People", MicroNed Netherlands

17. Brij Mohan, Ramesh S Arunachalam, Vinod Jain and NN Sharma, (2006b), "Micro-Enterprise Challenge Fund (MECF) Design Study for CORDAID", CORDAID, Netherlands
18. Y S P Thorat and Ramesh S Arunachalam-(2005), "Regulation And Areas Of Potential Market Failure In Micro-Finance", Paper Presented at NABARD High Level Policy Conference, New Delhi
19. Arunachalam Ramesh S (2005) "A Comprehensive MIS Toolkit for Financial Services Delivery for Low Income People: A Step by Step Guide for Implementation", MCG, India
20. Arunachalam Ramesh S (2001) "Designing and Implementing an MIS for Micro-finance: Key Strategies and Guidelines", Paper presented at SIDBI–BIRD Annual Conference and published as a chapter in book by published by BIRD (Bankers Institute of Rural Development)

Published Articles Related To Regulation/ Supervision, Governance, Digitization and Financial Stability

1. Arunachalam, Ramesh (2013), 'Should the RBI be made more accountable?—Part1', October 17, 2013, *Moneylife*, https://www.moneylife.in/article/should-the-rbi-be-made-more-accountable-mdashpart1/34926.html
2. Arunachalam, Ramesh (2013), 'How the RBI can be made more accountable – Part 2', October 24, 2013, *Moneylife*, https://www.moneylife.in/article/how-the-rbi-can-be-made-more-accountable-ndash-part-2/34996.html
3. Arunachalam, Ramesh (2013), 'How the RBI can be made more accountable— Part 3', October 31, 2013, *Moneylife*, https://www.moneylife.in/article/how-the-rbi-can-be-made-more-accountablemdash-part-3/35110.html
4. Arunachalam, Ramesh S (2012), 'Effective control systems at MIVs: The key to accountable investing and responsible microfinance globally', 10/09/2012, *Moneylife*, http://www.moneylife.in/article/effective-control-systems-at-mivs-the-key-to-accountable-investing-and-responsible-microfinance-globally/28376.html
5. Arunachalam, Ramesh S (2012), 'Regulation and supervision of microfinance investment vehicles: A suggested practical framework—Part I', 05/09/2012, *Moneylife*, http://www.moneylife.in/article/regulation-and-supervision-of-microfinance-investment-vehicles-a-suggested-practical-frameworkmdashpart-i/28284.html
6. Arunachalam, Ramesh S (2012), 'Regulation and supervision of microfinance investment vehicles: A suggested practical

framework—Part II', 06/09/2012, *Moneylife*, http://www.moneylife.in/article/regulation-and-supervision-of-microfinance-investment-vehicles-a-suggested-practical-frameworkmdash-part-ii/28314.html

7. Arunachalam, Ramesh S (2012), 'Why not regulate and supervise microfinance investment vehicles in their country of incorporation?', 20/08/2012, *Moneylife*, http://www.moneylife.in/article/why-not-regulate-and-supervise-microfinance-investment-vehicles-in-their-country-of-incorporation/27871.html

8. Arunachalam, Ramesh S (2012), 'Regulation and supervision of MIVs: An urgent task for central banks and regulators globally', 28/07/2012, *Moneylife*, http://www.moneylife.in/article/regulation-and-supervision-of-mivs-an-urgent-task-for-ral-banks-and-regulators-globally/27327.html

9. Arunachalam, Ramesh S (2012), 'Independent internal audit is the key to implementing responsible microfinance in MFIs', 12/07/2012, *Moneylife*, http://www.moneylife.in/article/independent-internal-audit-is-the-key-to-implementing-responsible-microfinance-in-mfis/26953.html

10. Arunachalam, Ramesh S (2012), 'How to make the boards of large NBFC MFIs implement corporate governance norms in practice? (Part I)', 04/07/2012, *Moneylife*, http://www.moneylife.in/article/how-to-make-the-boards-of-large-nbfc-mfis-implement-corporate-governance-norms-in-practice-part-i/26776.html

11. Arunachalam, Ramesh S (2012), 'Corporate governance: What boards of large NBFC MFIs can do on the ground? (Part II)', 09/07/2012, *Moneylife*, http://www.moneylife.in/article/corporate-governance-what-boards-of-large-nbfc-mfis-can-do-on-the-ground-part-ii/26865.html

12. Arunachalam, Ramesh S (2012), 'Critical risk and issues in regulating bank business correspondents', 16/06/2012, *Moneylife*, http://www.moneylife.in/article/critical-risk-and-issues-in-regulating-bank-business-correspondents/26335.html

13. Arunachalam, Ramesh S (2011), 'Priority sector lending to MFIs—need for adequate supervision, December 08, 2011, *Moneylife*, http://www.moneylife.in/article/priority-sector-lending-to-mfismdashneed-for-adequate-supervision/22060.html

14. Arunachalam, Ramesh S (2011), 'The special category of NBFC MFIs: Lessons for the Department of Non-Bank Supervision,

RBI' December 03, 2011, *Moneylife*, http://www.moneylife.in/article/the-special-category-of-nbfc-mfis-lessons-for-the-department-of-non-bank-supervision-rbi/21973.html

15. Arunachalam, Ramesh S (2011), 'Who Should Regulate Indian Microfinance?', November 16, 2011, *Moneylife*, http://www.moneylife.in/article/who-should-regulate-indian-micro-finance/21500.html
16. Arunachalam, Ramesh S (2011), 'MFI corporate governance norms: How can these be put in place?', September 30, 2011, *Moneylife*, http://www.moneylife.in/article/mfi-corporate-governance-norms-how-can-these-be-put-in-place/20223.html
17. Arunachalam, Ramesh S (2011), 'Establishing standards for effective management information systems for MFIs', September 12, 2011, *Moneylife*, http://www.moneylife.in/article/establishing-standards-for-effective-management-information-systems-for-mfis/19655.html
18. Arunachalam, Ramesh S (2011), 'Microfinance institutions should be permitted to transform into banks as it will help them improve services and reduce costs', August 31, 2011, *Moneylife*, http://www.moneylife.in/article/microfinance-institutions-should-be-permitted-to-transform-into-banks-as-it-will-help-them-improve-services-and-reduce-costs/19381.html
19. Arunachalam, Ramesh S (2011), 'Can the marriage of MFIs with banks be a sustainable option out of the microfinance crisis?', August 24, 2011, *Moneylife*, http://www.moneylife.in/article/can-the-marriage-of-mfis-with-banks-be-a-sustainable-option-out-of-the-microfinance-crisis/19176.html
20. Arunachalam, Ramesh S (2011), 'Never waste a crisis: Some suggested incentives for the proposed microfinance bill', August 19, 2011, *Moneylife*, http://www.moneylife.in/article/never-waste-a-crisis-some-suggested-inives-for-the-proposed-microfinance-bill/19073.html
21. Arunachalam, Ramesh S (2011), 'Four ways to improve the regulation of compensation at MFIs', August 02, 2011, *Moneylife*, http://www.moneylife.in/article/four-ways-to-improve-the-regulation-of-compensation-at-mfis/18585.html
22. Arunachalam, Ramesh S (2011), 'Who is an independent director? Who should be treated as an independent director in NBFC MFIs?', July 29, 2011, *Moneylife*, http://www.moneylife.in/article/who-is-an-independent-director-who-should-be-treated-as-an-independent-director-in-nbfc-mfis/18517.html

23. Arunachalam, Ramesh S (2011), 'Establish standards for MFI independent directors as first step to ensure good corporate governance', July 23, 2011, *Moneylife*, http://www.moneylife.in/article/establish-standards-for-mfi-independent-directors-as-first-step-to-ensure-good-corporate-governance/18328.html
24. Arunachalam, Ramesh S (2011), 'Increasing frauds, internal lapses at MFIs: Need to strengthen supervisory arrangements to protect the poor', July 22, 2011, *Moneylife*, http://www.moneylife.in/article/increasing-frauds-internal-lapses-at-mfis-need-to-strengthen-supervisory-arrangements-to-protect-the-poor/18309.html
25. Arunachalam, Ramesh S (2011), 'Does a five-star board guarantee good corporate governance?', July 20, 2011, *Moneylife*, http://www.moneylife.in/article/does-a-five-star-board-guarantee-good-corporate-governance/18239.html

Published In *Moneylife* Magazine (Web Version). He has over 50 plus articles at *Moneylife* and other places. Several of these pertain to improving governance and accountability as also regulatory and supervisory capacities of central banks.

Appendix 2B

Select Bibliography

1. Arunachalam, Ramesh S, "An Idea Which Went Wrong: Commercial Microfinance in India", Published by CreateSpace, 2014
2. Arunachalam, Ramesh S, "The Journey of Indian Micro-Finance: Lessons for the Future", Published by Aapti Publications, 2011.
3. Arunachalam, Ramesh S, "Financial Inclusion of Agriculture: Key Challenges and Ways Ahead for Agricultural Finance", Edited by Ms Smita Premchander, DFID WORLP Project, 2009.
4. Arunachalam, Ramesh S, and Vipin Sharma, "Marketing, Technology and Finance Constraints Related to MSMEs in India: A Status Report of 32 Sectors", Prepared for the National Commission on Enterprises in the Unorganized Sector (NCEUS), Government of India, 2009.
5. Arunachalam, Ramesh S, "Microfinance and Innovative Financing for Gender Equality: Approaches, Challenges and Strategies", 8th Women's Affairs Ministers Meeting (WAMM), Uganda, Published by Commonwealth Secretariat, 2008.
6. Arunachalam, Ramesh S, Kurian Katticaren, V Swarup and Kalpana Iyer, "Enhancing Financial Services Flow to Small Scale Marine Fisheries Sector—A Study for FAO/UNTRS", Published by FAO/UNTRS, 2008.
7. Arunachalam, Ramesh S, "Delivering Vulnerability Reducing Financial Services in an Inclusive Manner: Lessons from Commonwealth Countries for Building A Sustainable and Responsive Microfinance Portfolio", Commonwealth Secretariat and Govt. of Singapore (Paper Presented at Singapore) 2008.
8. Arunachalam, Ramesh S, "Microfinance and Innovative Financing for Gender Equality: Approaches, Challenges and Strategies, for 8 WAMM Commonwealth Ministers Meeting", Uganda, 2008.
9. Arunachalam Ramesh S, et al, "Microfinance and Economic Security: Towards a New Financial Inclusion Paradigm", Paper presented at the South Asia International Economic Security Conference, February 17 – 20th, 2008 New Delhi, 2008.

10. Arunachalam, Ramesh S, "Scoping Paper on Financial Inclusion: Considerations and Recommendations for UNDP", Published by UNDP, January 2008.
11. Arunachalam, Ramesh S, "UNDP Financial Inclusion Strategy in 7 Focus States: Strategic Consideration and Suggestions", UNDP, 2008.
12. Arunachalam Ramesh S et al, "Urban Poverty, MSMEs, Livelihoods and Microfinance: Critical Issues, Challenges and Strategies for Future", Paper presented at the Urban Poverty International Conference, January 21st – 22nd, 2008.
13. Arunachalam, Ramesh S, "Revisiting the Financial Inclusion Paradigm: A Review and Operationalization", MCG Working Paper, Chennai, 2007.
14. Arunachalam, Ramesh S, "Bamako 2000: Innovations in Microfinance", Technical Note 5

Key Articles
1. Abraham, Bobins, 'Currency Demonetisation Spikes Up Gold Prices, Government Eyes Clampdown', November 11, 2016, India Times, http://www.indiatimes.com/news/india/currency-demonetisation-spikes-up-gold-prices-government-eyes-clampdown-265293.html
2. Acharya, Shankar, 'How will Modi fix the terrifying jobs crisis?', December 03, 2019, Business Standard, https://www.rediff.com/business/column/how-will-modi-fix-the-terrifying-jobs-crisis/20191203.htm
3. Ahluwalia, Harveen, 'Farmers of Odisha go digital', February 15, 2016, Livemint, http://www.livemint.com/Politics/wHiHYViu0X4Q9nsDsZeH lL/Farmers-of-Odisha-go-digital.html
4. Allirajan, M., 'India's currency-GDP ratio highest among BRICS nations', November 23, 2016, The Times of India, http://timesofindia.indiatimes.com/business/india-business/Indias-currency-GDP-ratio-highest-among-BRICS-nations/articleshow/55576351.cms
5. Alm, James, Patricia Annez, and Arbind Modi, 'Stamp Duties in Indian States: A Case for Reform', September 2004, World Bank Policy Research Working Paper 3413, http://documents.worldbank.org/curated/en/775111468750283848/pdf/WPS3413.pdf
6. Amadeo, Kimberly, 'India's Economy, Its Challenges, Opportunities, and Impact', July 03, 2019, https://www.thebalance.com/india-s-economy-3306348

7. ANI, 'RCEP will be third big jolt to economy by PM Modi: Jairam Ramesh', October 25, 2019, https://economictimes.indiatimes.com/news/politics-and-nation/rcep-will-be-third-big-jolt-to-economy-by-pm-modi-jairam-ramesh/articleshow/71762852.cms?from=mdr
8. *ASSOCHAM* and *PWC*, 'Evolution of e-commerce in India: Creating the bricks behind the clicks', August 2014, http://www.pwc.in/assets/pdfs/publications/2014/evolution-of-e-commerce-in-india.pdf
9. Anwer, Javed, 'After demonetisation, e-wallets strike it rich while India runs out of cash', November 23, 2016, India Today, http://indiatoday.intoday.in/technology/story/after-demonetisation-e-wallets-strike-it-rich-while-india-runs-out-of-cash/1/817932.html
10. Babu, Gireesh, 'Jewellery industry hit by mandatory PAN Card for purchases over Rs 2 lakh', June 13, 2016, Business Standard, http://www.business-standard.com/article/companies/jewellery-industry-hit-by-mandatory-pan-card-for-purchases-over-rs-2-lakh-116061300696_1.html
11. Basu, Kaushik, 'India and the Mistrust Economy', November 6, 2019, https://www.nytimes.com/2019/11/06/opinion/india-economy.html
12. Bakshi, Ishan, 'Bharat has 70% of population, but only 19% of ATMs', November 28, 2016, Business Standard, http://www.rediff.com/business/report/note-scrapping-19-of-atms-for-70-of-population/20161128.htm
13. Beniwal, Vrishti, 'India goes postal in quest to open bank accounts for the masses', January 07, 2016, Livemint, http://www.livemint.com/Industry/mJ1bj7eb4K3uVs6ocLW84N/India-goes-postal-in-quest-to-open-bank-accounts-for-the-mas.html
14. Bhan, Shereen, 'Indians declare Rs 3,770cr under black money amnesty scheme', October 03, 2015, Money Control, http://www.moneycontrol.com/news/cnbc-tv18-comments/indians-declare-rs-3770cr-under-black-money-amnesty-scheme_3383781.html
15. Bhalla, Sahil, 'India's jugaad: Modi's demonetisation brings back the ancient barter system', November 15, 2016, http://www.catchnews.com/india-news/india-s-jugaad-modi-s-demonetisation-brings-back-the-ancient-barter-system-1479148760.html
16. Bhatia, Taru, 'Is India headed towards becoming a cashless economy?', November 9, 2016, Governance Now,

http://www.governancenow.com/news/regular-story/-india-headed-wards-becoming-a-cashless-economy

17. Bhatnagar, Gaurav Vivek, 'Digital Transactions Up By 100% Since Demonetisation, Says NPCI CEO', November 27, 2016, *The Wire,* http://thewire.in/82872/digital-transactions-up-by-100-since-demonetisation-says-ncpi-ceo/
18. BS Web Team, 'One week after demonetisation announcement, crores of old currency notes burned, destroyed, dumped', November 16, 2016, Business Standard, http://www.business-standard.com/article/current-affairs/demonetisation-effect-one-week-after-announcement-crores-old-currency-notes-burned-destroyed-dumped-116111600335_1.html
19. BS Web Team, 'The great Indian jugaad: How some are beating the Rs 1,000 note ban', November 11, 2016, Business Standard, http://www.business-standard.com/article/economy-policy/the-great-indian-jugaad-how-some-are-beating-the-rs-1000-note-ban-116111100406_1.html
20. Business Wire, 'Indian Government Announces FDI in Real Estate to Benefit the Real Estate Growth', November 17, 2015, The Hindu Business Line, http://www.thehindubusinessline.com/news/real-estate/indian-government-announces-fdi-in-real-estate-to-benefit-the-real-estate-growth/article7886880.ece
21. Chakravarty, Praveen, 'Viewpoint: How serious is India's economic slowdown?', August 27, 2019, https://www.bbc.com/news/world-asia-india-49470466
22. Chatterji, Rohini, 'Rural Economy Collapsing, Farmers In Trouble Because Of Demonetisation, Says BJP MP From Porbandar', November 16, 2016, Huffington Post, http://www.huffingtonpost.in/2016/11/15/rural-economy-collapsing-farmers-in-trouble-because-of-demoneti/
23. Chitravanshi, Ruchika, 'Government asks Paytm, Oxigen wallet to digitise rural cash', November 21, 2016, The Economic Times, http://economictimes.indiatimes.com/news/economy/finance/government-asks-paytm-oxigen-wallet-to-digitise-rural-cash/articleshow/55531592.cms
24. Das, Koustav, 'Make or break: Why next 2 months will be crucial for Indian economy', September 4, 2019, India Today, https://www.indiatoday.in/news-analysis/story/indian-economy-slowdown-revival-measures-next-two-months-crucial-1595216-2019-09-04
25. Daniyal, Shoaib, 'Even as common man is stuck in bank lines, raids have unearthed Rs 160 crores of new currency notes',

December 26, 2016, Scroll.in,
http://scroll.in/article/823912/even-as-common-man-is-stuck-in-bank-lines-raids-have-unearthed-rs-160-crores-of-new-currency-notes
26. Dave, Hiral, 'Amid banknotes chaos, 'digital' village that turned cashless is an oasis of calm', November 12, 2016, Hindustan Times, http://www.hindustantimes.com/india-news/amid-banknotes-chaos-digital-village-that-turned-cashless-is-an-oasis-of-calm/story-BRMwBCXMR7MGMiZs8dG8bM.html
27. Deccan Chronicle, 'Demonetisation: Tokens to ease Kukatpally Rythu Bazaar 'change' woes', November 19, 2016, http://www.deccanchronicle.com/nation/current-affairs/191116/demonetisation-tokens-to-ease-kukatpally-rythu-bazaar-change-woes.html
28. Dubey, Yogesh, and Aditya Dev, 'Dead since birth, Jan Dhan accounts now flush with cash', November 12, 2016, The Economic Times, http://economictimes.indiatimes.com/industry/banking/finance/banking/dead-since-birth-jan-dhan-accounts-now-flush-with-cash/articleshow/55385716.cms
29. Economist.com, 'The muddle Modi made-Narendra Modi is damaging India's economy as well as its democracy', October 24, 2019, https://www.economist.com/leaders/2019/10/24/narendra-modi-is-damaging-indias-economy-as-well-as-its-democracy
30. Editorial Staff, 'Indian Telecom Stats: 1 Billion Mobile Subscriber Base Reached, Active Base Cross 902M', January 5, 2016, Trak.in, http://trak.in/tags/business/2016/01/05/indian-telecom-stats-1billion-mobile-subscriber-base/
31. ET Bureau, 'Will risk even my life but will not give up the fight against black money: PM Narendra Modi', November 14, 2016, The Economic Times, http://economictimes.indiatimes.com/news/politics-and-nation/emotional-modi-asks-india-for-50-days-to-streamline-currency-spike/articleshow/55400961.cms
32. Economictimes.Com, 'Modi government applies more curbs, limits bank exchange from Rs 4,500 to Rs 2000', November 17, 2016, The Economic Times, http://economictimes.indiatimes.com/news/economy/policy/modi-government-applies-more-curbs-limits-bank-exchange-from-rs-4500-to-rs-2000/articleshow/55470284.cms
33. Express News Service, 'PM Modi reminds tax defaulters of September 30 deadline', June 27, 2016, The Indian Express, http://indianexpress.com/article/india/india-news-india/pm-

narendra-modi-mann-ki-baat-black-money-tax-evasion-undisclosed-assets-2877963/
34. Ghose, Debobrat, 'Narendra Modi's decision to curb fake currency inflow was a calculated strategy', November 9, 2016, *First Post*, http://www.firstpost.com/india/narendra-modis-decision-to-curb-fake-currency-inflow-was-a-calculated-strategy-3096460.html
35. India Brand Equity Foundation (IBEF), 'Real Estate Industry in India', July, 2016, http://www.ibef.org/industry/real-estate-india.aspx
36. ICICI Securities, 'E-payments: Revolutionary transformation in the Indian payment system', December 28 - January 01, 2016, http://content.icicidirect.com/mailimages/Payments.htm
37. Income Tax Department, 'Clarifications on the Income Declaration Scheme, 2016', June 30, 2016, Circular No. 25 of 2016, Government of India, Ministry of Finance, Department of Revenue Central Board of Direct Taxes, http://www.incometaxindia.gov.in/communications/circular/circular252016.pdf
38. India Today Web Desk, 'Gross Domestic Product growth falls to 4.5% in Q2 of 2019-20', November 29, 2019, https://www.indiatoday.in/business/story/gross-domestic-product-growth-falls-4-5-per-cent-q2-2019-20-1623733-2019-11-29
39. Indo-Asian News Service *(IANS)*, 'Demonetisation: Black money calculations don't add up, Modi government may be in for a shock', December 1, 2016, First Post, http://www.firstpost.com/business/demonetisation-black-money-calculations-dont-add-up-modi-government-may-be-in-for-a-shock-3134338.html
40. Indo-Asian News Service *(IANS)*, 'Currency Press Capacity: Around 6 Months Needed To Replenish Rs. 500 Notes', November 17, 2016, *NDTV*, http://www.ndtv.com/india-news/currency-press-capacity-around-6-months-needed-to-replenish-rs-500-notes-1626660
41. Indo-Asian News Service *(IANS)*, 'Banks have enough cash for exchange of demonetised notes: RBI', November 11, 2016, http://www.business-standard.com/article/economy-policy/banks-have-enough-cash-for-exchange-of-demonetised-notes-rbi-116111100936_1.html
42. Indo-Asian News Service *(IANS)*, 'Online shoppers in India to cross 100 million by 2016: Study', November 20, 2014, Gadgets Now, http://www.gadgetsnow.com/tech-news/Online-

shoppers-in-India-to-cross-100-million-by-2016-Study/articleshow/45217773.cms
43. Indo-Asian News Service *(IANS)*, 'India to overtake US in smartphones by 2016', India in Business, http://indiainbusiness.nic.in/newdesign/index.php?param=newsdetail/10367
44. Jacob, Rahul, 'Why it's still difficult to do business in India', December 05, 2019, Business Standard, Rediff, https://www.rediff.com/business/column/why-its-still-difficult-to-do-business-in-india/20191205.htm
45. Jaffrelot, Christophe, 'Indian direct investment', June 29, 2015, The Indian Express, http://indianexpress.com/article/opinion/columns/indian-direct-investment/
46. Jagannathan, R, 'Why Jaitley's threats won't work: All black money is in stock markets & real estate, too risky to touch', October 5, 2015, First Post, http://www.firstpost.com/business/why-jaitleys-threats-will-not-work-all-black-money-is-in-stock-markets-real-estate-too-risky-to-touch-2454746.html
47. Jain, Mayank, 'Yes, India has massive income inequality—but it isn't the second-most unequal country in the world', September 06, 2016, Scroll.in, http://scroll.in/article/815751/yes-india-has-massive-income-inequality-but-it-isnt-the-second-most-unequal-country-in-the-world
48. Jaleel, Tania Kishore, 'Why cash is still king for Indian consumers', April 20 2016, Livemint, http://www.livemint.com/Money/jCjgdI36iBHWt30hN3gOSP/Why-cash-is-still-king-for-Indian-consumers.html
49. Jha, Dilip Kumar, 'Farmers are worried despite high onion prices', December 12, 2019, Business Standard, Rediff, https://www.rediff.com/business/report/farmers-are-worried-despite-high-onion-prices/20191212.htm
50. Jha, Dilip Kumar, 'Gold, silver prices surge as reaction to demonetisation and Trump win', November 10, 2016, Business Standard, http://www.business-standard.com/article/markets/gold-silver-prices-surge-as-reaction-to-demonetisation-and-trump-win-116110901265_1.html
51. Kapoor, Amit, 'The dynamics of India's growth slowdown', September 09, 2019, IANS, https://economictimes.indiatimes.com/news/economy/indicators/the-dynamics-of-indias-growth-recession/articleshow/71020942.cms?from=mdr

52. Kayal, Rajesh M, 'Why the govt's new income declaration schemes are different from the amnesties of earlier times', July 21, 2016, The Indian Express, http://indianexpress.com/article/explained/black-money-declarants-income-declaration-scheme-dispute-resolution-scheme-amnesty-schemes-pm-modi-2926436/
53. Khullar, Rahul, 'How will you revive economy, Mr Modi?', December 19, 2019, Business Standard, Rediff.com, https://www.rediff.com/business/column/how-will-you-revive-economy-mr-modi/20191219.htm
54. Lalwani, Ashok, 'This is how India can become the next Silicon Valley', October 02, 2019, https://www.weforum.org/agenda/2019/10/india-technology-development-silicon-valley/
55. Livemint.com, 'Fundamentals of Indian economy continue to be strong; Q3 GDP may pick up: CEA', November 29, 2019, https://www.livemint.com/news/india/fundamentals-of-indian-economy-continue-to-be-strong-q3-gdp-may-pick-up-cea-11575038409083.html
56. Livemint, 'Cash crunch: Analysts cut India GDP growth forecast', November 24, 2016, http://www.livemint.com/Politics/gG3pF45hFU53GyXE1BwIuJ/Cash-crunch-Analysts-cut-India-GDP-growth-forecast.html
57. Livemint, 'India one of the most cash intensive economies', November 15, 2016, http://www.livemint.com/Money/CVkOV1emoQwCNXh0TZPyKI/India-one-of-the-most-cash-intensive-economies.html
58. Maiti, Subhendu, 'Cash crunch: Howrah wholesale fish market on the verge of closure', November 17, 2016, Hindustan Times, http://www.hindustantimes.com/kolkata/cash-crunch-howrah-wholesale-fish-market-on-the-verge-of-closure/story-zD3wmksCSIPuSyjXmT6vkO.html
59. Mampatta, Sachin P, 'Companies with worst corporate governance scores', December 19, 2019, Business Standard, Rediff.com, https://www.rediff.com/business/report/companies-with-worst-corporate-governance-scores/20191219.htm
60. Mishra, Asit Ranjan, 'RCEP deal hangs in balance even as India, other members resolve some issues', October 26, 2019, Livemint, https://www.livemint.com/news/world/rcep-deal-hangs-in-balance-even-as-india-other-members-resolve-some-issues-11572065771510.html
61. Mishra, Asit Ranjan, 'India has started linking Jan Dhan scheme, Aadhaar and mobile numbers: Arun Jaitley', April 02, 2016,

Livemint, http://www.livemint.com/Politics/PRmaclHkzL6fGJEUIVLo3H/India-has-started-linking-Jan-Dhan-scheme-Aadhaar-and-mobil.html

62. Mishra, Lalatendu, 'E-wallet firms' customer base surges', November 25, 2016, The Hindu, http://www.thehindu.com/business/E-wallet-firms%E2%80%99-customer-base-surges/article16695644.ece

63. Modak, Samie, 'Why markets remain unfazed despite GDP shocker', December 19, 2019, Business Standard, Rediff.com, https://www.rediff.com/business/report/why-markets-remain-unfazed-despite-gdp-shocker/20191219.htm

64. Mohan, Archis, 'GST compensation: States plan political battle over delayed allocation', December 09, 2019, Business Standard, Rediff, https://www.rediff.com/business/report/gst-compensation-states-get-battle-ready/20191209.htm

65. Mohan, Archis and Sanjeeb Mukherjee 'NITI Aayog on how India can become $5-trillion economy', December 02, 2019, Business Standard, Rediff, https://www.rediff.com/business/report/niti-aayog-on-how-india-can-become-5-trillion-economy/20191202.htm

66. Money Control News, 'FM Nirmala Sitharaman to address media at 3:15 pm today', December 13, 2019, https://www.moneycontrol.com/news/business/economy/fm-nirmala-sitharaman-to-address-media-at-315-pm-today-4726931.html

67. Moss, Daniel, 'View: With growth this bad, India needs more than luck', November 30, 2019, Bloomberg, https://economictimes.indiatimes.com/news/economy/policy/with-growth-this-bad-india-needs-more-than-luck/articleshow/72302855.cms

68. Nair, Smita, See 'The Un-real Estate: The sector that is going to take the biggest hit', November 13, 2016, The Indian Express, http://indianexpress.com/article/india/india-news-india/the-un-real-estate-demonetisation-process-100-500-rupee-note-narendra-modi-black-money-4372286/

69. Nair, Remya, 'PAN made mandatory for all transactions above Rs2 lakh', December 18, 2015, Livemint, http://www.livemint.com/Politics/UkFNyKXvjG8oE3QxzSM6bI/PAN-compulsory-for-opening-all-bank-accountsm-says-revenue.html

70. PRSIndia.org, The Benami Transactions (Prohibition) Amendment Act, 2016, No. 43 Of 2016, August 10, 2016, Ministry Of Law And Justice, The Gazette of India',

http://www.prsindia.org/uploads/media/Benami/Benami%20Transactions%20Act,%202016.pdf
71. Press Information Bureau, 'The Income Declaration Scheme 2016 to open from 1st June 2016', May 14, 2016, Government of India, Ministry of Finance, http://pib.nic.in/newsite/PrintRelease.aspx?relid=145360
72. Paliath, Shreehari, 'The muddle Modi made Narendra Modi is damaging India's economy as well as its democracy', November 3, 2019, https://www.indiaspend.com/there-are-very-strong-concerns-about-the-indian-economy/
73. Pathak, Tarun, 'India Smartphone Market Grew 23% Amid Flat Global Annual Growth', April 29, 2016, Counterpoint Technology Market Research, http://www.counterpointresearch.com/india1q16/
74. Pratheesh, 'Demonetisation to hit terror financing hard', November 10, 2016, The Hindu, http://www.thehindu.com/news/national/demonetisation-to-hit-terror-financing-hard/article9325696.ece
75. Pal, Deepali, '8 Major Problems Faced by the Indian Economy', http://www.economicsdiscussion.net/indian-economy/problems-indian-economy/8-major-problems-faced-by-the-indian-economy/14140
76. Pandey, Kundan, 'Experts warn about the dangers of signing RCEP', October 16, 2019, https://www.downtoearth.org.in/news/agriculture/experts-warn-about-the-dangers-of-signing-rcep-67283
77. Pandey, Ashish 'Hyderabad: Onion wholesale market closed due to cash crunch in wake of demonetisation', November 16, 2016, India Today, Posted by Ankit Misra, http://indiatoday.intoday.in/story/hyderabad-onion-wholesale-market-demonetisation-of-500-1000-rupee-notes-cash-crunch/1/811913.html
78. Pandit, Virendra, 'No cash, no worries for this 'digital' village', November 24, 2016, The Hindu Business Line, http://www.thehindubusinessline.com/news/national/demonetisation-no-cash-no-worries-for-this-digital-village/article9381737.ece
79. Press Information Bureau, 'The Income Declaration Scheme 2016 to open from 1st June 2016', May 14, 2016, Government of India, Ministry of Finance, http://pib.nic.in/newsite/PrintRelease.aspx?relid=145360

80. *PMINDIA*, 'PM's address to the Nation', November 8, 2016, http://www.pmindia.gov.in/en/news_updates/prime-ministers-address-to-the-nation/?comment=disable
81. Preetha, M. Soundariya, 'SBI to finish ATM recalibration soon', November 24, 2016, The Hindu, http://www.thehindu.com/business/Industry/SBI-to-finish-ATM-recalibration-soon/article16695634.ece
82. Press Trust of India, 'Fitch cuts India's FY20 growth forecast to 4.6%', December 20, 2019, Rediff.com, https://www.rediff.com/business/report/fitch-cuts-indias-fy20-growth-forecast-to-46/20191220.htm
83. Press Trust of India, 'Industry needs to come out of 'self doubt' mood: Sitharaman', December 20, 2019, Rediff.com, https://www.rediff.com/business/report/industry-needs-to-come-out-of-self-doubt-mood-fm/20191220.htm
84. Press Trust of India, 'PM exhorts India Inc to take bold investment decisions', December 20, 2019, Rediff.com, https://www.rediff.com/business/report/modi-goes-all-out-to-pacify-corporate-india/20191220.htm
85. Press Trust of India, 'Gita Gopinath on why India needs to keep fiscal deficit target', December 20, 2019, Rediff.com, https://www.rediff.com/business/report/india-needs-to-keep-fiscal-deficit-target-gopinath/20191220.htm
86. Press Trust of India, 'Budget: TUs want FM to hike I-T ceiling, minimum wages, pension', December 19, 2019, https://www.rediff.com/business/report/budget-tus-want-fm-to-hike-i-t-ceiling-to-rs-10-lakh/20191219.htm
87. Press Trust of India, 'At $73 bn, deal activities see a sharp 40% drop', December 19, 2019, https://www.rediff.com/business/report/at-73-bn-deal-activities-see-a-sharp-40-drop/20191219.htm
88. Press Trust of India, 'India Inc draws govt attention on ease of doing business', December 19, 2019, Rediff.com, https://www.rediff.com/business/report/india-inc-draws-attention-on-ease-of-doing-business/20191219.htm
89. Press Trust of India, 'FMCG players stare at low growth of 9-10% this year', December 18, 2019, Rediff.com, https://www.rediff.com/business/report/fmcg-players-stare-at-low-growth-of-9-10-this-year/20191218.htm
90. Press Trust of India, 'Budget 2020: What states want from Sitharaman', December 18, 2019, Rediff.com, https://www.rediff.com/money/report/budget-2020-what-states-want-from-sitharaman/20191218.htm

91. Press Trust of India, 'Average wealth expectancy of affluent Indians is just Rs 3.6 cr: Report', December 18, 2019, Rediff.com, https://www.rediff.com/business/report/average-wealth-expectancy-of-rich-indians-is-rs-36-cr/20191218.htm
92. Press Trust of India, 'Exports contract for 4th straight month in Nov', December 13, 2019, Rediff, https://www.rediff.com/business/report/more-bad-news-exports-down-for-4th-straight-month/20191213.htm
93. Press Trust of India, 'GST rates may go up for various items', December 11, 2019, Rediff, https://www.rediff.com/business/report/gst-rates-may-go-up-for-various-items/20191211.htm
94. Press Trust of India, 'More bad news, Goldman pegs FY20 GDP growth at 5.3%', December 03, 2019, https://www.rediff.com/business/report/more-bad-news-goldman-pegs-fy20-gdp-growth-to-53/20191203.htm
95. Press Trust of India, 'Indian economy currently facing challenges, says Sitharaman', November 10, 2019, https://economictimes.indiatimes.com/news/economy/policy/indian-economy-currently-facing-challenges-says-sitharaman/articleshow/71996526.cms?from=mdr
96. Press Trust of India, 'Economic slowdown: GST collections dip to 19-month low of Rs 91,916 crore in September', October 1, 2019, https://www.indiatoday.in/business/story/economic-slowdown-gst-collections-dip-to-19-month-low-of-rs-91-916-crore-in-september-1605265-2019-10-01
97. Press Trust of India, 'On November 8, RBI had only Rs 4.94 lakh crore in 2000 rupee notes: RTI', December 19, 2016, The Economic Times, http://economictimes.indiatimes.com/news/economy/finance/on-november-8-rbi-had-only-rs-4-94-lakh-crore-in-2000-rupee-notes-rti/articleshow/56065299.cms
98. Press Trust of India, 'No estimation of black money either before or after November 8: FM Arun Jaitley', December 16, 2016, The Economic Times, http://economictimes.indiatimes.com/news/economy/finance/no-estimation-of-black-money-either-before-or-after-november-8-fm-arun-jaitley/articleshow/56019908.cms
99. Press Trust of India, 'Jewellers unhappy over mandatory PAN on purchase of Rs 2 lakh' December 16, 2015, The Economic Times, http://economictimes.indiatimes.com/wealth/personal-finance-news/jewellers-unhappy-over-mandatory-pan-on-purchase-of-rs-2-lakh/articleshow/50207202.cms

100. Press Trust of India, 'Income Tax Act amendment a 'win-win', to boost govt revenues: Experts', November 28, 2016, The Indian Express, http://indianexpress.com/article/india/india-news-india/income-tax-act-amendment-a-win-win-to-boost-govt-revenues-experts/
101. Press Trust of India, 'Demonetization: 'Housing prices already at lowest, no scope for correction,' says CREDAI', November 27, 2016, Daily News and Analysis (DNA), http://www.dnaindia.com/money/report-demonetization-housing-prices-already-at-lowest-no-scope-for-correction-says-credai-2277276
102. Press Trust of India, 'PM Modi pushes for use of mobiles to deal with cash crunch', November 25, 2016, The Times of India, http://timesofindia.indiatimes.com/india/PM-Modi-pushes-for-use-of-mobiles-to-deal-with-cash-crunch/articleshow/55618832.cms
103. Press Trust of India, 'Demonetisation: Housing prices to drop up to 30%, wiping Rs 8 lakh cr in value', November 24, 2016, First Post, http://www.firstpost.com/business/demonetisation-housing-prices-to-drop-up-to-30-wiping-rs-8-lakh-cr-in-value-3122946.html
104. Press Trust of India, 'Demonetisation: Misuse of bank account for black money deposit to invite govt action', November 24, 2016, The Indian Express, http://indianexpress.com/article/india/india-news-india/demonetisation-government-to-prosecute-jan-dhan-account-holders-for-black-money-deposit-4382373/
105. Press Trust of India, 'Demonetisation: Misuse of bank account for black money deposit to invite govt action', November 24, 2016, The Indian Express, http://indianexpress.com/article/india/india-news-india/demonetisation-government-to-prosecute-jan-dhan-account-holders-for-black-money-deposit-4382373/
106. Press Trust of India, 'Latest on demonetisation: No debit card charges and other developments', November 23, 2016, The Tribune, http://www.tribuneindia.com/news/nation/latest-on-demonetisation-debit-card-charges-dropped-and-other-relaxations/327296.html
107. Press Trust of India, 'Government allows farmers to buy seeds with old Rs 500 notes', November 21, 2016, The Economic Times, http://economictimes.indiatimes.com/news/economy/agriculture/government-allows-farmers-to-buy-seeds-with-old-rs-500-notes/articleshow/55539367.cms

108. Press Trust of India, 'Don't hoard currency, sufficient notes in supply: RBI', November 17, 2016, Deccan Herald, http://www.deccanherald.com/content/581579/dont-hoard-currency-sufficient-notes.html
109. Press Trust of India, 'Slash stamp duty to clean up real estate sector: Assocham', November 14, 2016, The Economic Times, http://economictimes.indiatimes.com/wealth/real-estate/slash-stamp-duty-to-clean-up-real-estate-sector-assocham/articleshow/55413511.cms?from=mdr
110. Press Trust of India, 'India overtakes China, becomes biggest gold consumer: Survey', October 27, 2015, The Economic Times, http://economictimes.indiatimes.com/news/economy/indicators/india-overtakes-china-becomes-biggest-gold-consumer-survey/articleshow/49556979.cms
111. Press Trust of India, 'Only 3.6% households go in for cashless dealings: Report', September 6, 2013, The Times of India, http://timesofindia.indiatimes.com/business/india-business/Only-3-6-households-go-in-for-cashless-dealings-Report/articleshow/22370847.cms
112. Press Trust of India, '30% of India's real estate sector funded by black money', June 06, 2016, The Economic Times Realty, http://realty.economictimes.indiatimes.com/news/industry/30-of-indias-real-estate-sector-funded-by-black-money/52614378
113. Press Trust of India, 'India's black economy shrinking, pegged at 20% of GDP: Report', June 5, 2016, The Indian Express, http://indianexpress.com/article/business/economy/ambit-capital-black-economy-shrinking-pegged-at-20-per-cent-of-gdp-2835783/
114. Raghavan, T C A Srinivasa, 'Is Modi going the Manmohan way?', December 05, 2019, https://www.rediff.com/business/column/is-modi-going-the-manmohan-way/20191205.htm
115. Radhakrishna, GS, 'Demonetisation: Why Chandrababu Naidu is the only non-BJP CM to hail move', November 18, 2016, First Post, http://www.firstpost.com/politics/demonetisation-why-chandrababu-naidu-is-the-only-non-bjp-cm-to-hail-move-3111644.html
116. Rai, Siddhartha, 'Poor people become black money mules for rich', November 13, 2016, India Today, Posted by Anand, Jayaram, http://indiatoday.intoday.in/story/poor-black-money-mules-rich/1/809457.html
117. Rai, Dipu, 'IT dept to swoop down on tax evaders in stock market', October 13, 2016, Daily News and Analysis (DNA),

http://www.dnaindia.com/money/report-rs-30-lakh-crore-black-money-in-stock-markets-i-t-2263647

118. RBI Press Release, 'Shri R. Gandhi and Shri S. S. Mundra, RBI Deputy Governors brief Agencies on Currency Issues: Edited Transcript', December 13, 2016, https://rbi.org.in/Scripts/BS_PressReleaseDisplay.aspx?prid=38886
119. RBI, 'RBI Bulletin', November 10, 2016, https://rbi.org.in/scripts/BS_ViewBulletin.aspx?Id=16609
120. RBI Press Release, 'Mobile Payments in India - Operative Guidelines for Banks', June 12, 2008, https://rbidocs.rbi.org.in/rdocs/PressRelease/PDFs/84979.pdf
121. RBI, 'Concept Paper on Card Acceptance Infrastructure', April 15, 2016, Department of Payment and Settlement Systems, https://rbidocs.rbi.org.in/rdocs/PublicationReport/Pdfs/MDRDBEDA36AB77C4C81A3951C4679DAE68F.PDF
122. RBI Press Release, 'RBI Seeks Feedback on Concept Paper on Card Acceptance Infrastructure', March 08, 2016, https://www.rbi.org.in/Scripts/BS_PressReleaseDisplay.aspx?prid=36427
123. Rediff.com, 'Indian economy headed for ICU: India's ex-CEA', December 18, 2019, http://news.rediff.com/commentary/2019/dec/18/indian-economy-headed-for-icu-indias-excea/82f97e02e0fc61fd87a61cf8435b0802
124. Rediff.com, 'Crisil sharply cuts FY20 growth forecast to 5.1%', December 02, 2019, https://www.rediff.com/business/report/crisil-sharply-cuts-fy20-growth-forecast-to-51/20191202.htm
125. Rediff.com, 'GDP growth sputters to 4.5%, weakest in over 6 years', November 29, 2019, https://m.rediff.com/money/report/crisis-deepens-q2-gdp-growth-slips-to-45/20191129.htm
126. Rediff.com, 'GDP is expected to pick up in Q3, says CEA Subramanian', November 29, 2019, https://www.rediff.com/business/report/gdp-is-expected-to-pick-up-in-q3-says-cea-subramanian/20191129.htm
127. Rediff.com, 'Core sector output shrinks by 5.8% in October', November 29, 2019, https://www.rediff.com/business/report/core-sector-output-shrinks-by-58-in-october/20191129.htm
128. Reuters, 'How A Trusted Bureaucrat Led The Top Secret Demonetisation Project In Two Rooms At Modi's Delhi Residence', December 9, 2016, Huffington Post,

http://www.huffingtonpost.in/2016/12/08/how-a-trusted-bureaucrat-led-the-top-secret-demonetisation-proje/

129. Reuters, 'How Modi and team kept demonetisation a closely guarded secret', December 09, 2016, The Hindu, http://www.thehindu.com/news/national/How-Modi-and-team-kept-demonetisation-a-closely-guarded-secret/article16782821.ece

130. Rogoff, Kenneth, 'Costs and benefits to phasing out paper currency', April 11, 2014, Presented at NBER Macroeconomics Annual Conference, http://scholar.harvard.edu/files/rogoff/files/c13431.pdf

131. Roychoudhury, Arup, 'Govt set to miss FY20 fiscal deficit target', December 18, 2019, Business Standard, Rediff.com, https://www.rediff.com/business/report/govt-set-to-miss-fy20-fiscal-deficit-target/20191218.htm

132. Roy, Anup, 'Soon, RTGS facility may be available 24X7', December 18, 2019, Business Standard, Rediff.com, https://www.rediff.com/business/report/soon-rtgs-facility-may-be-available-24x7/20191218.htm

133. Sahani, Vidushi, 'Benami Transactions (Prohibition) Amendment Act, 2016 To Come In To Effect From Tomorrow [Read Bill]', October 31, 2016, LiveLaw.in, http://www.livelaw.in/benami-transactions-prohibition-amendment-act-2016-come-effect-tomorrow-read-bill/

134. Sapam, Bidya, 'Opinion divided over impact of demonetisation on real estate prices', November 21, 2016, Livemint, http://www.livemint.com/Companies/o2fVwCBoD8rrJv12XaENmL/Opinion-divided-over-impact-of-demonetisation-on-real-estate.html

135. Sarang, Bindisha and BV Rao, 'Demonetisation: PM Modi aborted plan to calibrate ATMs for Rs 100 notes. Why?', November 19, 2016, First Post, http://www.firstpost.com/business/demonetisation-pm-modi-aborted-plan-to-calibrate-atms-for-rs-100-notes-why-3112020.html

136. Sen, Pronab, 'Modi's Demonetisation Move May Have Permanently Damaged India's Informal Sector', November 16, 2016, The Wire, http://thewire.in/80564/modis-demonetisation-move-may-have-permanently-damaged-indias-informal-sector/

137. Sen, Sudhi Ranjan, 'Indian Air Force's Biggest Aircraft Are Now Ferrying Tonnes Of Currency Across India', November 29, 2016, The Huffington Post,

http://www.huffingtonpost.in/2016/11/28/indian-air-forces-biggest-aircraft-are-now-ferrying-tonnes-of-c/
138. Seth, Dilasha, and Indivjal Dhasmana 'GST: Decision on ITC may hit cash flow, fears India Inc', December 20, 2019, Business Standard, Rediff.com, https://www.rediff.com/business/report/gst-decision-on-itc-may-hit-cash-flow-says-india-inc/20191220.htm
139. Singh, Rajiv, 'Demonetisation: Why the challenge to take digital payment to rural India is as huge as the opportunity', November 27, 2016, The Economic Times, http://economictimes.indiatimes.com/news/economy/policy/sunday-et-making-rural-india-pay-digitally-and-challenges-post-demonetisation/articleshow/55640316.cms
140. Singha, Rajib, 'Indian Businesses Lost $4 Billion Due to Cyberattacks in 2013; 2014 to be Worse', December 19, 2014, Quick Heal Blog, http://blogs.quickheal.com/indian-businesses-lost-4-billion-due-cyberattacks-2013-2014-worse/
141. Sinha, Sanjeev, 'Budget 2019: Should there be no income tax in India? Here's what tax experts say', July 4, 2019, Financial Express, https://www.financialexpress.com/budget/budget-2019-should-there-be-no-income-tax-in-india-heres-what-tax-experts-say/1626855/
142. Shaikh, Zeeshan, 'Recovery of fake notes dipped by 30 per cent between 2013 & 2015: Fake became too 'original' to detect', November 13, 2016, The Indian Express, http://indianexpress.com/article/india/india-news-india/recovery-of-fake-notes-dipped-by-30-per-cent-between-2013-2015-fake-became-too-original-to-detect-4372414/
143. Shankar, B V Shiva, 'Parallel economy: Jan-Dhan accounts used to launder money', November 15, 2016, The Times of India, http://timesofindia.indiatimes.com/city/bengaluru/Parallel-economy-springsup-Jan-Dhan-accountsused-to-launder-money/articleshow/55423362.cms
144. Sharma, Swati Goel, 'A Delhi Trader Reveals How Touts Are Helping People Convert Their Black Cash Into New Notes', November 25, 2016, Scoop Whoop, https://www.scoopwhoop.com/A-Delhi-Trader-Reveals-How-Touts-Are-Converting-Peoples-Black-Money-Into-New-Notes/#.ub4wslv3b
145. Sharma, Mihir S, 'What Modi got wrong about the economy', December 18, 2019, Business Standard, Rediff.com, https://www.rediff.com/business/column/what-modi-got-wrong-about-the-economy/20191218.htm

146. Sharma, Ravi Teja, 'Private equity investments in realty rise 40 per cent to Rs 3,840 crore in March quarter', May 07, 2016, *The Economic Times*, http://economictimes.indiatimes.com/wealth/real-estate/private-equity-investments-in-realty-rise-40-per-cent-to-rs-3840-crore-in-march-quarter/articleshow/52159685.cms
147. Sharma, Ravi Teja, 'Real Estate Bill is an act now, may protect home buyers', May 02, 2016, The Economic Times, http://economictimes.indiatimes.com/wealth/real-estate/real-estate-bill-is-an-act-now-may-protect-home-buyers/articleshow/52069308.cms
148. Shukla, Saloni, and Pratik Bhakta, '3.2 million debit cards compromised; SBI, HDFC Bank, ICICI, YES Bank and Axis worst hit', October 20, 2016,The Economic Times, http://economictimes.indiatimes.com/industry/banking/finance/banking/3-2-million-debit-cards-compromised-sbi-hdfc-bank-icici-yes-bank-and-axis-worst-hit/articleshow/54945561.cms
149. Sridhar, G Naga, 'RuPay card transactions jump from four lakh/day to 10 lakh', November 22, 2016, The Hindu Business Line, http://www.thehindubusinessline.com/money-and-banking/rupay-card-transactions-jump-from-four-lakhday-to-10-lakh/article9374656.ece
150. Toppr, 'Development Issues of Indian Economy', https://www.toppr.com/guides/business-economics-cs/overview-of-indian-economy/development-issues-of-indian-economy/
151. The Financial Express, '59 demonetisation changes before 50 days: Here are 10 important developments', December 20, 2016, http://www.financialexpress.com/economy/59-demonetisation-changes-before-50-days-here-are-10-important-developments/480212/
152. The Financial Express, 'Demonetisation: You can use your old Rs 500 notes at petrol pumps and airline counters only till December 2', December 1, 2016, http://www.financialexpress.com/industry/banking-finance/demonetisation-rbi-cuts-rs-500-notes-validity-to-dec-2-from-dec-15-at-petrol-pumps-and-airline-counters/461044/
153. The Financial Express, 'Demonetisation: 'Emotional' PM Narendra Modi vows, "This is just the beginning, more to come"', November 22, 2016, http://www.financialexpress.com/india-news/demonetisation-pm-narendra-modi-vows-this-is-just-the-beginning-more-to-come/452372/

154. The Hindu Business Line, 'Reforms in real estate key to GDP growth: Credai', January 6, 2013, http://www.thehindubusinessline.com/news/real-estate/reforms-in-real-estate-key-to-gdp-growth-credai/article4279859.ece
155. The Hindu 'GST revenues not enough for States' compensation: Centre', December 05, 2019, https://www.thehindu.com/business/Economy/gst-revenues-not-enough-for-states-compensation-centre/article30152551.ece
156. The Hindu, 'Rs. 65,250 cr. mopped up via new black money window', November 01, 2016, http://www.thehindu.com/news/national/black-money-rs-65250-crore-disclosed-under-income-declaration-scheme-says-arun-jaitley/article9173242.ece
157. The Hindu, 'Demonetisation cripples fishing industry in Bengal', November 25, 2016, http://www.thehindu.com/news/cities/kolkata/demonetisation-cripples-fishing-industry-in-bengal/article9340809.ece
158. The Indian Express, 'Currency demonetisation: CM Devendra Fadnavis asks urban local bodies to keep payment counters open today', November 14, 2016, http://indianexpress.com/article/india/india-news-india/currency-demonetisation-cm-devendra-fadnavis-asks-urban-local-bodies-to-keep-payment-counters-open-today-4373880/
159. The Times of India, "Notes' replace notes in Mizoram village', November 16, 2016, http://timesofindia.indiatimes.com/city/guwahati/Notes-replace-notes-in-Mizoram-village/articleshow/55451270.cms
160. TRAI Information Note to the Press, 'Telecom Regulatory Authority Of India (TRAI)', July 29, 2016, Press Release No. 74/2016, http://www.trai.gov.in/WriteReadData/PressRealease/Document/Press_Release_No74_Eng_29_july_2016.pdf
161. University of Pennsylvania Almanac, 'Taxes in the Ancient World', December 2, 2016, http://www.upenn.edu/almanac/v48/n28/AncientTaxes.html
162. Varma, Subodh, 'Queues of pain for tiny gain on black money?', November 21, 2016, The Times of India, http://timesofindia.indiatimes.com/india/Queues-of-pain-for-tiny-gain-on-black-money/articleshow/55532113.cms
163. Varma, Subodh, 'Jan Dhan scorecard: 22 cr bank accounts opened, average balance Rs 1,725', May 26, 2016, The Times of India, http://timesofindia.indiatimes.com/india/Jan-Dhan-

scorecard-22-cr-bank-accounts-opened-average-balance-Rs-1725/articleshow/52442488.cms
164. Venkatesan, Rashmi, 'Demonetisation Isn't an 'Inconvenience', It's a Gross Violation of Our Rights', November 20, 2016, The Wire, http://thewire.in/81364/demonetisation-rights-violation/
165. Venkatesh, Mahua, 'Misuse of bank account for black money deposit to invite govt action', November 18, 2016, Hindustan Times, http://www.hindustantimes.com/india-news/misuse-of-bank-account-for-black-money-deposit-to-invite-govt-action/story-NmqcCcCsz5pmJGy2E1oHGJ.html
166. Vita, Stephen, '3 Economic Challenges for India in 2019', May 24, 2019, Investopedia, https://www.investopedia.com/articles/investing/012516/3-economic-challenges-india-faces-2016.asp
167. *VISA,* 'Accelerating The Growth of Digital Payments in India: A Five - Year Outlook', October, 2016, http://www.visa.co.in/aboutvisa/research/include/Digital_Payments_India.pdf
168. Vyas, Hitesh, 'A year of Shaktikanta Das: The hits & misses as RBI guv', December 11, 2019, PTI, Rediff.com, https://www.rediff.com/business/report/a-year-of-shaktikanta-das-hits--misses-as-rbi-guv/20191211.htm
169. Waghmare, Abhishek, 'Promised GST revenue to states may get trimmed', December 19, 2019, Business Standard, Rediff.com, https://www.rediff.com/business/report/gst-promised-gst-revenue-to-states-may-get-trimmed/20191219.htm
170. Waghmare, Abhishek, 'Explained in Charts: Indian economy loses sheen', December 03, 2019, Business Standard, https://www.rediff.com/business/report/explained-in-charts-indian-economy-loses-sheen/20191203.htm
171. Waghmare, Abhishek, 'Indian economy loses sheen amid slowdown: Explained in seven charts', December 1, 2019, https://www.business-standard.com/article/economy-policy/indian-economy-loses-sheen-amid-slowdown-explained-in-seven-charts-119120100774_1.html
172. Warrier, Shobha 'India becoming 3rd largest economy is not far away', December 04, 2019, https://www.rediff.com/business/interview/india-becoming-3rd-largest-economy-is-not-far-away/20191204.htm
173. https://www.brbnmpl.co.in/english/
174. World Bank Financial Inclusion Database, 2014.

Appendix 3

United Nations' Sustainable Development Goals (UNSDGs) # 1 and 10[3]

Goal 1: End poverty in all its forms everywhere

Goal 1 Targets

- **1.1** By 2030, eradicate extreme poverty for all people everywhere, currently measured as people living on less than $1.25 a day

- **1.2** By 2030, reduce at least by half the proportion of men, women and children of all ages living in poverty in all its dimensions according to national definitions

- **1.3** Implement nationally appropriate social protection systems and measures for all, including floors, and by 2030 achieve substantial coverage of the poor and the vulnerable

- **1.4** By 2030, ensure that all men and women, in particular the poor and the vulnerable, have equal rights to economic resources, as well as access to basic services, ownership and control over land and other forms of property, inheritance, natural resources, appropriate new technology and financial services, including microfinance

- **1.5** By 2030, build the resilience of the poor and those in vulnerable situations and reduce their exposure and vulnerability

---

[3] Source: UNDP website, https://www.undp.org/content/undp/en/home/sustainable-development-goals.html

to climate-related extreme events and other economic, social and environmental shocks and disasters

- **1.A** Ensure significant mobilization of resources from a variety of sources, including through enhanced development cooperation, in order to provide adequate and predictable means for developing countries, in particular least developed countries, to implement programmes and policies to end poverty in all its dimensions
- **1.B** Create sound policy frameworks at the national, regional and international levels, based on pro-poor and gender-sensitive development strategies, to support accelerated investment in poverty eradication actions

Goal 10: Reduce inequality within and among countries

Goal 10 Targets
- **10.1** By 2030, progressively achieve and sustain income growth of the bottom 40 per cent of the population at a rate higher than the national average
- **10.2** By 2030, empower and promote the social, economic and political inclusion of all, irrespective of age, sex, disability, race, ethnicity, origin, religion or economic or other status
- **10.3** Ensure equal opportunity and reduce inequalities of outcome, including by eliminating discriminatory laws, policies and practices and promoting appropriate legislation, policies and action in this regard
- **10.4** Adopt policies, especially fiscal, wage and social protection policies, and progressively achieve greater equality

- **10.5** Improve the regulation and monitoring of global financial markets and institutions and strengthen the implementation of such regulations
- **10.6** Ensure enhanced representation and voice for developing countries in decision-making in global international economic and financial institutions in order to deliver more effective, credible, accountable and legitimate institutions
- **10.7** Facilitate orderly, safe, regular and responsible migration and mobility of people, including through the implementation of planned and well-managed migration policies
- **10.A** Implement the principle of special and differential treatment for developing countries, in particular least developed countries, in accordance with World Trade Organization agreements
- **10.B** Encourage official development assistance and financial flows, including foreign direct investment, to States where the need is greatest, in particular least developed countries, African countries, small island developing States and landlocked developing countries, in accordance with their national plans and programmes
- **10.C** By 2030, reduce to less than 3 per cent the transaction costs of migrant remittances and eliminate remittance corridors with costs higher than 5 per cent

Appendix 4

Note on Copyright Aspects

Ramesh S Arunachalam claims copyright only with the original writings, ideas, interpretation, and analysis done by the author, Ramesh S Arunachalam. No copyright is claimed with regard to any material that is quoted, which are any ways, very, very negligible. Furthermore, where quoted, material that is quoted has been paraphrased and cited appropriately—such quotes, which are negligible in comparative terms to the overall book, would anyways come under fair use policy. Where original quotes are used, they are primarily taken from Statutory Enquiry Commissions. All of these, to the best of my understanding and interpretation of the law, are free of copyright protection. In fact, as per the website of the Office of the Law Revision Counsel United States Code[4] and the website of the United States Copyright office,[5] as per Section, 105,. (Subject matter of copyright: United States Government works), copyright protection (under this title) is not available for any work of the United States Government.

That said, every document that has been quoted has been thoroughly checked for copyright information and none of the documents from which quotes have been taken contain copyright notice either as a symbol © (the letter C in a circle), or the word "Copyright," or the abbreviation "Copr."

There is no name of the owner, no abbreviation by which the name can be recognized, no generally known alternative designation of the owner, nor any indication of an owner of any copyright in these government works. Therefore, in the absence of the copyright notice

---

[4] Office of the Law Revision Counsel United States Code, 17 USC: Subject Matter of Copyright: United States Government works, http://uscode.house.gov/view.xhtml?req=%28title:17%20section:105%20edition:prelim%29

[5] Copyright Law of the United States of America and Related Laws Contained in Title 17 of the *United States Code*, Section 105, Subject Matter of Copyright: United States Government works, http://www.copyright.gov/title17/92chap1.html#105

and copyright owner information and as per Sections 105 and 403 of the Copyright Laws of the United States, it can only be inferred that these government reports, orders, releases etc. (representing work of the United States federal government), are not protected by copyright. Likewise, the concerned websites have either stated that "information on State Department websites is in the public domain and may be copied and distributed without permission,"[6] or they have stated that "all of the content of the website constitutes a work of the United States federal government under sections 105[7] and 403[8] of title 17 of the U.S. Code," which again frees the information from copyright protection.

---

[6] U.S. Department of State, Copyright Information, http://www.state.gov/misc/87529.htm#copyright

[7] Subject Matter of Copyright: United States Government works, U.S Code 105.

[8] Copyright Law of the United States of America and Related Laws Contained in Title 17 of the *United States Code,* Section 403, Notice of copyright: Publications incorporating United States Government works, http://www.copyright.gov/title17/92chap4.html

Appendix 5

The Revolving Door Phenomenon in the United States of America (USA) Prior to the 2008 Financial Crisis

One of the biggest reasons for weak regulatory systems, prior to the 2008 financial crisis, is the near seamless shift of key people from Wall Street and private sector to regulatory and supervisory bodies through the "reverse revolving door" phenomenon.

Top executives of Wall Street firms (and representatives of special interest groups including lobbyists) have been known to take up positions in the Government or the regulatory set up.

Paulson, for example, the Treasury Secretary of the United States during the years 2006–2009 is a classic case. He came to the Treasury after nearly thirty-two years at Goldman Sachs.

Robert Rubin is yet another of those who made the switch from Wall Street to government. It must be recalled here that much of the foundation for the de-regulation that took place during former President Bill Clinton's second term, was laid during Rubin's tenure. It is, of course, common knowledge what this de-regulation ultimately did in terms of repealing the Glass-Steagall Act, thereby resulting in the 2008 financial crisis.[9]

Often called "the reverse revolving door" phenomenon, these people have established a very strong pro-financial sector/Wall Street bias in policy formulation and regulatory enforcement by regulators and supervisors that oversee their (former) industry, former employers

---

[9] This is an opinion expressed in the final report of the Financial Crisis Enquiry Commission (FCIC), http://fcic-static.law.stanford.edu/cdn_media/fcic-reports/fcic_final_report_full.pdf

and/or related institutions. This oftentimes resulted in de-regulation to the detriment of the end user.

Second, is the shift of key people from government institutions to Wall Street and private sector through the normal revolving door phenomenon. There are the cases where key people from regulatory and supervisory bodies and governments have moved (either through a permanent or temporary relationship) to lucrative private-sector positions at Wall Street firms. Two examples are relevant here:
1. Paid speeches delivered by former Government position holders — all the Wall Street speeches by Hillary and Bill Clinton would come under this category; and
2. People like Lawrence Summers, Timothy Geithner, or Robert Rubin for that matter, who, after having served as Treasury Secretary, went on to work with Wall Street firms like D. E. Shaw, Warburg Pincus,[10] and Citigroup respectively.

Third, there have also been situations where former decision makers (including policy makers and executive decision makers) have become paid advocates and use their knowledge of and connections with governmental agencies, regulators, and supervisors to advance the interests of Wall Street companies. This again would be part of Wall Street lobbying. All of these have created significant conflicts of interests prior to the 2008 financial crisis and have been an important reason for the financial crisis having occurred itself.

---

[10] A Wall Street private equity firm

Appendix 6

The 2008 Financial Crisis in The United States of America

If there is one thing that stands out about the 2008 financial crisis in the USA, it is the fact that weak, lax and laissez-faire regulation—caused by lobbying, PACs, campaign financing, and the power of Wall Street to influence policy makers, regulators and others—served as an important factor that triggered the meltdown. There are no two opinions on this and this is what the Financial Crisis Inquiry Commission (FCIC) Final Report[11] dated January 2011 has said over and over again. If one looks closely at many of the past financial crisis situations (like the 2008 global financial crisis fueled by the U.S. sub-prime and other crisis situations before that), it is clear that they can be linked to lax and laissez-faire regulatory and supervisory frameworks. Frameworks that were either developed by industry insiders with commercial interests or created with significant input from such insiders—both with a view to benefit the overall financial industry concerned.

In other words, these regulatory and supervisory frameworks had serious "conflict of interest situations" that led to such lax and laissez-faire regulatory and supervisory frameworks being developed in the first place. In effect, they were regulating their own industry. There can be no doubt that this was corruption at its worst, caused by inherent conflicts of interests that were at play.

Despite all that has happened, even today, there is a puzzling lack of attention given to the role played by conflicts of interest in the corruption saga and especially with regard to the larger financial sector. Look at the United Nations Convention Against Corruption (UNCAC). Even the UNCAC only makes a fleeting mention of the role played by conflicts of interests, despite it being the important

---

[11] Financial Crisis Inquiry Report, Final Report Of The National Commission On The Causes Of The Financial And Economic Crisis In The United States, The Financial Crisis Inquiry Commission, 2011, http://fcic-static.law.stanford.edu/cdn_media/fcic-reports/fcic_final_report_full.pdf

keystone to unearthing corruption and supporting the structure to fight against corruption worldwide.

It is not just my opinion; many scholars, academics, economists, politicians, and business people worldwide also agree that the close regulation and monitoring of conflicts of interest are of great importance to regulatory ethics. Moreover, this is something that all of us need to note with urgency because, if not eliminated, these conflict of interest situations could spell disaster for the larger financial sector as they will inevitably lead to corruption, and, ultimately, to financial crisis caused by laissez-faire regulation and supervision.

That said, let us now look at what is meant[12] by "conflict of interest." A "conflict of interest" is a conflict between the duty, roles, responsibilities, and private interests of any official that could improperly and unfairly influence the performance of his/her official roles and responsibilities. By private interests, I mean the following: Private interests include financial, pecuniary and other interests[13] which generate a direct personal benefit to the public official as also personal affiliations, associations, and family ties, that could (practically be considered as likely to) improperly and unfairly influence the official's performance of his/her roles, duties and responsibilities.

Defined in this way, conflict of interest has the potential to undermine the proper functioning of institutions (public, private, not-for-profit), governments and the like by:
- Weakening adherence by officials to the ideals of impartiality, objectivity, fairness, and legitimacy, in decision making, and

---

[12] These definitions have been compiled from several sources including OECD and other material found on the web, which are far too numerous to quote. These are gratefully and sincerely acknowledged.

[13] The negotiation of future employment by an official (for himself/family/friends) prior to his leaving his present office is one example here and there are many more examples that I could provide. This is like negotiating a job with a vendor. For example, an official may say, "I will make rules governing X and Y situations very lenient provided you make my nephew the CEO in another project of yours."

- Distorting the rule of law, the development and application of policy, the functioning of organizations and markets, as well as the allocation of resources.

Indeed, what is the difference between conflict of interest and corruption?

Conflict of interest situations exist where officials, because of their position, have the *opportunity* to abuse the power and authority of their position for personal and private gain. On the other hand, corruption exists where officials *have abused* their position for personal and private gain. Put differently, conflicts of interest situations do not always lead to corruption. However, where there is corruption, you can be sure that conflicts of interest indeed exist. Why do we need to attach so much importance to conflicts of interest with regard to regulation and supervision in the financial sector? Because if conflicts of interest are not eliminated and/or at least properly monitored by independent bodies, or reduced, the situation can easily lead to corruption in regulation and supervision and thereby threaten the entire financial system.

This is not new. This is what past crisis situations have taught us. In fact, if there is a single most recurring theme in financial crises and scandals globally, it is the failure to manage conflicts of interest. The following are some well-known examples. Let us look this with regard to the larger financial sector in the United States, which provides a very useful lesson with regard to conflicts of interest and their relationship to crisis situations.

As described[14] by former SEC Chairman Arthur Levitt:

> Bank involvement in the securities markets came under close scrutiny after the 1929 market crash. The Pecora hearings of 1933 ...uncovered a wide range of abusive practices on the part of banks and bank affiliates. These included a variety of conflicts of interest; the underwriting of unsound securities in order to pay off bad bank loans; and "pool operations" to support the price of bank stocks.

---

[14] Testimony of Arthur Levitt, Chairman U.S. Securities and Exchange Commission,
http://www.sec.gov/news/testimony/testarchive/1995/spch029.txt

In fact, as Levitt has further argued,[15] and please note this carefully, it is the significant revelations of "uncontrolled conflicts of interest" that provided the basis and rationale for the passing of many subsequent regulations—the Securities Act (1933), the Securities Exchange Act (1934), and the Glass-Steagall Banking Act (1933). In fact, it appears that conflicts of interest were also the major reason for the enactment of the Investment Company Act (1940) and the Investment Advisor Act (1940).

Closer to the 1990s, I see numerous examples of conflicts of interest that led directly to the financial crisis:
- The insider trading scandals (such as, the Ivan Boesky and Dennis Levine scandals in the 1980s), the closure of Drexel Burnham Lambert (the investment bank) and the associated (criminal) conviction of its famous employee (Michael Milken) are still fresh in my memory.
- Later, there were more financial scandals in the early 2000s—for example, the internet bubble in 2000/2001 exposed problems with dubious high-flying research analysts (with significant conflicts of interest), whose reports were in fact, influenced by their own institutions' investment banking interests. This, in fact, led to specific provisions in the Sarbanes-Oxley Act that dealt with conflicts of interest among research analysts.
- Then, just over a decade ago, in 2003, the SEC found that the use of brokerage commissions to facilitate the sales of fund shares [was] widespread among funds that relied on broker-dealers to sell fund shares. This led to the adoption of new rules to prohibit funds from this practice.[16]
- Then, even closer to home, we had the mother of all financial crises in recent times—the global financial crisis of 2008—which was again based on significant conflicts of interest in many areas and I quote from the FCIC report hereafter which identifies several key aspects that caused the 2008 financial crisis, including conflicts of interest.

---

[15] Ibid.
[16] Please see: Prohibition on the Use of Brokerage Commissions to Finance Distribution, Investment Company Act Release 26591 (Sept. 2, 2004), 69 Fed. Register 54728, 54728 (Sept. 9, 2004), http://www.sec.gov/rules/final/ic-26591.pdf

First Cause

The first key point from the FCIC report is given below:

> The captains of finance and the public stewards of our financial system ignored warnings and failed to question, understand, and manage evolving risks within a system essential to the well-being of the American public. Theirs was a big miss, not a stumble. ...
>
> The prime example is the Federal Reserve's pivotal failure to stem the flow of toxic mortgages, which it could have done by setting prudent mortgage-lending standards. The Federal Reserve was the one entity empowered to do so and it did not. The record of our examination is replete with evidence of other failures: financial institutions made, bought, and sold mortgage securities they never examined, did not care to examine, or knew to be defective; firms depended on tens of billions of dollars of borrowing that had to be renewed each and every night, secured by subprime mortgage securities; and major firms and investors blindly relied on credit rating agencies as their arbiters of risk. What else could one expect on a highway where there were neither speed limits nor neatly painted lines? (FCIC Report, Page no 17)[17]

The reader will note the emphasis on the "pivotal failure" of the regulator—the Federal Reserve. The reader will also note that the FCIC report mentions the fact that:

> Financial institutions made, bought, and sold mortgage securities they never examined, did not care to examine, or knew to be defective; firms depended on tens of billions of dollars of borrowing that had to be renewed each and every night, secured by subprime mortgage securities; and major

---

[17] Financial Crisis Inquiry Report, Final Report Of The National Commission On The Causes Of The Financial And Economic Crisis In The United States, The Financial Crisis Inquiry Commission, 2011, http://fcic-static.law.stanford.edu/cdn_media/fcic-reports/fcic_final_report_full.pdf

> firms and investors blindly relied on credit rating agencies as their arbiters of risk. (FCIC Report, Page no 17)[18]

And surely, as the FCIC report argues in the next point (given below), law/policy makers and regulators, for reasons best known to them, did have a huge say in creating such a "highway where there were neither speed limits nor neatly painted lines"[19] and where reckless driving was the norm (rather than the exception).

Given the above, you will now understand why it is important that current as well as future law and policy-makers and politicians who participate in the American electoral process, especially for the office of the President of the United States, must come clean on their relationships with Wall Street firms. There should be no question about this.

Second Cause

Let us move to the next key point identified by the FCIC:

> We conclude widespread failures in financial regulation and supervision proved devastating to the stability of the nation's financial markets. The sentries were not at their posts, in no small part due to the widely accepted faith in the self-correcting nature of the markets and the ability of financial institutions to effectively police themselves. More than 30 years of deregulation and reliance on self-regulation by financial institutions, championed by former Federal Reserve chairman Alan Greenspan and others, supported by successive administrations and Congresses, and actively pushed by the powerful financial industry at every turn, had stripped away key safeguards, which could have helped avoid catastrophe. This approach had opened up gaps in oversight of critical areas with trillions of dollars at risk, such as the shadow banking system and over-the-counter derivatives markets. In addition, the government permitted financial firms to pick their preferred regulators in what became a race to the weakest supervisor. ...

---

[18] Financial Crisis Inquiry Report, Final Report Of The National Commission On The Causes Of The Financial And Economic Crisis In The United States, The Financial Crisis Inquiry Commission, 2011, http://fcic-static.law.stanford.edu/cdn_media/fcic-reports/fcic_final_report_full.pdf
[19] Ibid.

> Changes in the regulatory system occurred in many instances as financial markets evolved. Nevertheless, as the report will show, the financial industry itself played a key role in weakening regulatory constraints on institutions, markets, and products. It did not surprise the Commission that an industry of such wealth and power would exert pressure on policy makers and regulators. From 1999 to 2008, the financial sector expended $2.7 billion in reported federal lobbying expenses; individuals and political action committees in the sector made more than $1 billion in campaign contributions. What troubled us was the extent to which the nation was deprived of the necessary strength and independence of the oversight necessary to safeguard financial stability. (FCIC Report, Page no 18)[20]

Please note the comment on the failure of financial regulation and supervision in causing the crisis as well as the reference to lobbying expenses, campaign contributions and the power and wealth of Wall Street to "exert pressure on policy makers and regulators." For a moment I thought that it was Bernie Sanders who had written this report but I was mistaken. These words appear in the final report of the FCIC, the Statutory Commission that inquired into the Financial Crisis of 2008. Now, tell me whether, as an American, you feel comfortable when a potential law/policy maker talks of reining in Wall Street but refuses to release the paid speeches that she made to a key Wall Street firm like Goldman Sachs, which has been repeatedly cited in the FCIC report.

Third Cause

Alright, let us move on to the next point cited by FCIC and it is about self-regulation — an idea sold by large Wall Street Firms, Financial Conglomerates, Big Banks and Corporations to Law/Policy Makers and Regulators, who readily bought this idea and faced the consequences via the financial crisis of 2008:

---

[20] Financial Crisis Inquiry Report, Final Report Of The National Commission On The Causes Of The Financial And Economic Crisis In The United States, The Financial Crisis Inquiry Commission, 2011, http://fcic-static.law.stanford.edu/cdn_media/fcic-reports/fcic_final_report_full.pdf

We conclude dramatic failures of corporate governance and risk management at many systemically important financial institutions were a key cause of this crisis. There was a view that instincts for self-preservation inside major financial firms would shield them from fatal risk-taking without the need for a steady regulatory hand, which, the firms argued, would stifle innovation. Too many of these institutions acted recklessly, taking on too much risk, with too little capital, and with too much dependence on short-term funding. In many respects, this reflected a fundamental change in these institutions, particularly the large investment banks and bank holding companies, which focused their activities increasingly on risky trading activities that produced hefty profits. They took on enormous exposures in acquiring and supporting subprime lenders and creating, packaging, repackaging, and selling trillions of dollars in mortgage-related securities, including synthetic financial products. Like Icarus,[21] they never feared flying ever closer to the sun.

Many of these institutions grew aggressively through poorly executed acquisition and integration strategies that made effective management more challenging. The CEO of Citigroup told the Commission that a $40 billion position in highly rated mortgage securities would "not in any way have excited my attention," and the co-head of Citigroup's investment bank said he spent "a small fraction of 1%" of his time on those securities. In this instance, too big to fail meant too big to manage.

Financial institutions and credit rating agencies embraced mathematical models as reliable predictors of risks, replacing judgment in too many instances. Too often, risk management became risk justification.

---

[21] In Greek mythology, Icarus is the son of the master craftsman Daedalus, the creator of the Labyrinth. Icarus and his father attempted to escape from Crete by means of wings that his father had constructed from feathers and wax. Icarus's father warns him first of complacency and then of hubris, asking that he fly neither too low nor too high, so the sea's dampness would not clog his wings or the sun's heat melt them. Icarus ignored his father's instructions not to fly too close to the sun, whereupon the wax in his wings melted and he fell into the sea.

Compensation systems—designed in an environment of cheap money, intense competition, and light regulation—too often rewarded the quick deal, the short-term gain—without proper consideration of long-term consequences. Often, those systems encouraged the big bet—where the payoff on the upside could be huge and the downside limited. This was the case up and down the line—from the corporate boardroom to the mortgage broker on the street.

Our examination revealed stunning instances of governance breakdowns and irresponsibility. You will read, among other things, about AIG senior management's ignorance of the terms and risks of the company's $79 billion derivatives exposure to mortgage-related securities; Fannie Mae's quest for bigger market share, profits, and bonuses, which led it to ramp up its exposure to risky loans and securities as the housing market was peaking; and the costly surprise when Merrill Lynch's top management realized that the company held $55 billion in "super-senior" and supposedly "super-safe" mortgage-related securities that resulted in billions of dollars in losses. (FCIC Report, Page no 18 and 19)[22]

Yet the law/policy makers and regulators swore by self-regulation. Why were they so dogmatic and shortsighted? Self-regulation is an oxymoron and has never worked ... ever! It pushes people to fly like Icarus who did not fear flying closer to the sun and simply perished. Now, this again, is a clear failure on the part of policy and law-makers who were convinced by these large Wall Street firms, financial conglomerates, banks and corporations to bring in the paradigm of self-regulation as a key component of the regulatory and supervisory process. Again, as before, the cost of this decision was very high and it resulted in the financial crisis of 2008, the impact of which we are still feeling today.

---

[22] Financial Crisis Inquiry Report, Final Report Of The National Commission On The Causes Of The Financial And Economic Crisis In The United States, The Financial Crisis Inquiry Commission, 2011, http://fcic-static.law.stanford.edu/cdn_media/fcic-reports/fcic_final_report_full.pdf

Fourth, Fifth and Sixth Causes

The FCIC report talks of three more critical aspects that led to the financial crisis of 2008 and each of these is highlighted below:

> We conclude a combination of excessive borrowing, risky investments, and lack of transparency put the financial system on a collision course with crisis. Clearly, this vulnerability was related to failures of corporate governance and regulation, but it is significant enough by itself to warrant our attention here.
>
> In the years leading up to the crisis, too many financial institutions, as well as too many households, borrowed to the hilt, leaving them vulnerable to financial distress or ruin if the value of their investments declined even modestly. For example, as of 2007, the five major investment banks—Bear Stearns, Goldman Sachs, Lehman Brothers, Merrill Lynch, and Morgan Stanley—were operating with extraordinarily thin capital. By one measure, their leverage ratios were as high as 40 to 1, meaning for every $40 in assets, there was only $1 in capital to cover losses. Less than a 3% drop in asset values could wipe out a firm. To make matters worse, much of their borrowing was short-term, in the overnight market—meaning the borrowing had to be renewed each and every day. For example, at the end of 2007, Bear Stearns had $11.8 billion in equity and $383.6 billion in liabilities and was borrowing as much as $70 billion in the overnight market. It was the equivalent of a small business with $50,000 in equity borrowing $1.6 million, with $296,750 of that due each and every day. One can't really ask, "What were they thinking?" when it seems that too many of them were thinking alike. (FCIC Report, Page no 19 and 20)[23]

Anyone with financial sense will argue that such leverage is ridiculous, and yet it was consciously allowed by the powers that be. Where were regulators and law policy-makers? I don't know. No one seems to know!

---

[23] Financial Crisis Inquiry Report, Final Report Of The National Commission On The Causes Of The Financial And Economic Crisis In The United States, The Financial Crisis Inquiry Commission, 2011, http://fcic-static.law.stanford.edu/cdn_media/fcic-reports/fcic_final_report_full.pdf

We conclude over-the-counter derivatives contributed significantly to this crisis. The enactment of legislation in 2000 to ban the regulation by both the federal and state governments of over-the-counter (OTC) derivatives was a key turning point in the march toward the financial crisis. ...

OTC derivatives contributed to the crisis in three significant ways. First, one type of derivative—credit default swaps (CDS)—fueled the mortgage securitization pipeline. CDS were sold to investors to protect against the default or decline in value of mortgage-related securities backed by risky loans. Companies sold protection—to the tune of $79 billion, in AIG's case—to investors in these newfangled mortgage securities, helping to launch and expand the market and, in turn, to further fuel the housing bubble.

Second, CDS were essential to the creation of synthetic CDOs. These synthetic CDOs were merely bets on the performance of real mortgage-related securities. They amplified the losses from the collapse of the housing bubble by allowing multiple bets on the same securities and helped spread them throughout the financial system.

Goldman Sachs alone packaged and sold $73 billion in synthetic CDOs from July 1, 2004, to May 31, 2007. Synthetic CDOs created by Goldman referenced more than 3,400 mortgage securities, and 610 of them were referenced at least twice. This is apart from how many times these securities may have been referenced in synthetic CDOs created by other firms. ...

While financial institutions surveyed by the FCIC said they do not track revenues and profits generated by their derivatives operations, some firms did provide estimates. For example, Goldman Sachs estimated that between 25% and 35% of its revenues from 2006 through 2009 were generated by derivatives, including 70% to 75% of the firm's commodities business, and half or more of its interest rate and currencies business. From May 2007 through November 2008, $133 billion, or 86%, of the $155 billion of trades made by

Goldman's mortgage department were derivative transactions.[24] (FCIC Report, Page no 24, 25, 78 and 79)[25]

Here we go once again with another example where regulation was banned *by legislation* and as the FCIC report argues, and I quote, "the enactment of legislation in 2000 to ban the regulation by both the federal and state governments of over-the-counter (OTC) derivatives was a key turning point in the march toward the financial crisis."

Why on earth would the Federal Government ban regulation with legislation and thereby purchase a crisis? The answer eludes me. I simply don't understand why this happened or how it could happen. Was no one watching? Was it lobbying, friendly relationships between policy and law-makers with Wall Street firms, paid speeches, and/or campaign donations that did the trick? I'm not sure, and I simply cannot fathom why this banning of regulation happened in the year 2000.

> Removing barriers helped consolidate the banking industry. Between 1990 and 2005, 74 "megamergers" occurred involving banks with assets of more than $10 billion each. Meanwhile, the 10 largest jumped from owning 25% of the industry's assets to 55%. From 1998 to 2007, the combined assets of the five largest U.S. banks—Bank of America, Citigroup, JP Morgan, Wachovia, and Wells Fargo—more than tripled, from $2.2 trillion to $6.8 trillion.[26] And investment banks were growing bigger, too. Smith Barney acquired Shearson in 1993 and Salomon Brothers in 1997, while Paine Webber purchased Kidder, Peabody in 1995. Two years later, Morgan Stanley merged with Dean Witter, and Bankers Trust purchased Alex. Brown & Sons. The assets of the five largest investment banks —Goldman Sachs, Morgan Stanley, Merrill Lynch, Lehman

---

[24] FCIC Report (2011), Original Footnote 57: Data provided to the FCIC by Goldman Sachs.

[25] Financial Crisis Inquiry Report, Final Report Of The National Commission On The Causes Of The Financial And Economic Crisis In The United States, The Financial Crisis Inquiry Commission, 2011, http://fcic-static.law.stanford.edu/cdn_media/fcic-reports/fcic_final_report_full.pdf

[26] FCIC Report (2011), Original Footnote 2: These were the largest banks as of 2007. See FCIC, "Preliminary Staff Report: Too-Big-to-Fail Financial Institutions," August 31, 2010, p. 14.

Brothers, and Bear Stearns—quadrupled, from $1 trillion in 1998 to $4 trillion in 2007.[27]

In the spring of 1996, after years of opposing repeal of Glass-Steagall, the Securities Industry Association—the trade organization of Wall Street firms such as Goldman Sachs and Merrill Lynch—changed course. Because restrictions on banks had been slowly removed during the previous decade, banks already had beachheads in securities and insurance. Despite numerous lawsuits against the Fed and the OCC, securities firms and insurance companies could not stop this piecemeal process of deregulation through agency rulings.[28] Edward Yingling, the CEO of the American Bankers Association (a lobbying organization), said, "Because we had knocked so many holes in the walls separating commercial and investment banking and insurance, we were able to aggressively enter their businesses—in some cases more aggressively than they could enter ours. So first the securities industry, then the insurance companies, and finally the agents came over and said let's negotiate a deal and work together.[29] (FCIC Report, Page no 80, 81 and 82)[30]

In addition, the FCIC Report stated:

The new regime encouraged growth and consolidation within and across banking, securities, and insurance. The bank-centered financial holding companies such as Citigroup, JP Morgan, and Bank of America could compete directly with the

---

[27] FCIC Report (2011), Original Footnote 3: Data from SNL Financial (www.snl.com/).

[28] FCIC Report (2011), Original Footnote 12: Securities Industry Association v. Board of Governors of the Federal Reserve System, 627 F. Supp. 695 (D.D.C. 1986); Kathleen Day, "Reinventing the Bank; With Depression-Era Law about to Be Rewritten, the Future Remains Unclear," *Washington Post,* October 31, 1999.

[29] FCIC Report (2011), Original Footnote 13: Edward Yingling, quoted in "The Making of a Law," *ABA Banking Journal,* December 1999.

[30] Financial Crisis Inquiry Report, Final Report Of The National Commission On The Causes Of The Financial And Economic Crisis In The United States, The Financial Crisis Inquiry Commission, 2011, http://fcic-static.law.stanford.edu/cdn_media/fcic-reports/fcic_final_report_full.pdf

"big five" investment banks —Goldman Sachs, Morgan Stanley, Merrill Lynch, Lehman Brothers, and Bear Stearns—in securitization, stock and bond underwriting, loan syndication, and trading in over-the-counter (OTC) derivatives. The biggest bank holding companies became major players in investment banking. The strategies of the largest commercial banks and their holding companies came to more closely resemble the strategies of investment banks. Each had advantages: commercial banks enjoyed greater access to insured deposits, and the investment banks enjoyed less regulation. Both prospered from the late 1990s until the outbreak of the financial crisis in 2007. However, Greenspan's "spare tire" that had helped make the system less vulnerable would be gone when the financial crisis emerged—all the wheels of the system would be spinning on the same axle. (FCIC Report, Page no 84)[31]

Again, the above represents a classic case where, in the name of innovation and consolidation, regulatory safeguards were removed, resulting in the system being more vulnerable when the financial crisis actually emerged (as all the wheels of the system were indeed spinning on the same axle, which eventually broke under the load). Please note that, as the FCIC report argues very clearly, the financial crisis was essentially caused by a regulatory and policy failure that occurred because regulation and supervision were either lax and/or regulatory safeguards had been removed through lobbying, legislation and the like. We simply cannot afford more of this in the future. That is why, with the backdrop of the 2008 financial crisis (and its aftermath) and the role played by Wall Street (including investment banks, commercial banks, financial conglomerates etc.) in creating and sustaining this crisis, we simply cannot have presidential nominees cozy up to Wall Street and refuse to release transcripts of their paid for speeches. Sorry, but that is unacceptable and is not good electoral governance in any form or manner . . . anywhere!

---

[31] Financial Crisis Inquiry Report, Final Report Of The National Commission On The Causes Of The Financial And Economic Crisis In The United States, The Financial Crisis Inquiry Commission, 2011, http://fcic-static.law.stanford.edu/cdn_media/fcic-reports/fcic_final_report_full.pdf

Seventh Cause

Let's move on further and get to the governance of compensation, which played a very important role in the 2008 financial crisis. Indeed, compensation is one factor among many that contributed to the financial crisis in the United States, and elsewhere. Moreover, the FCIC report has also mentioned the same and this is quoted below:

> Both before and after going public, investment banks typically paid out half their revenues in compensation. For example, Goldman Sachs spent between 44% and 49% a year between 2005 and 2008, when Morgan Stanley allotted between 46% and 59%. Merrill paid out similar percentages in 2005 and 2006, but gave 141% in 2007—a year it suffered dramatic losses.[32]
>
> As the scale, revenue, and profitability of the firms grew, compensation packages soared for senior executives and other key employees. John Gutfreund, reported to be the highest-paid executive on Wall Street in the late 1980s, received $3.2 million in 1986 as CEO of Salomon Brothers.[33] Stanley O'Neal's package was worth more than $91 million in 2006, the last full year he was CEO of Merrill Lynch.[34] In 2007, Lloyd Blankfein, CEO ofat Goldman Sachs, received $68.5 million;[35] Richard Fuld, CEO of Lehman Brothers, and Jamie Dimon, CEO of JPMorgan Chase, received about $34 million and $28 million, respectively.[36] That year Wall Street paid workers in New York roughly $33 billion in year-end bonuses alone.[37]

---

[32] FCIC Report (2011), Original Footnote 63: Goldman Sachs, 2006 and 2009 10-K; Morgan Stanley, 2008 10-K; Merrill Lynch, 2005 and 2008 10-K.

[33] FCIC Report (2011), Original Footnote 64: "Gutfreund's Pay Is Cut," *New York Times,* December 23, 1987.

[34] FCIC Report (2011), Original Footnote 65: Merrill Lynch, "2007 Proxy Statement," p. 38.

[35] FCIC Report (2011), Original Footnote 66: Goldman Sachs, "Proxy Statement for 2008 Annual Meeting of Shareholders," March 7, 2008, p. 16: Blankfein received $600,000 base salary and a 2007 year-end bonus of $67.9 million.

[36] FCIC Report (2011), Original Footnote 67: Lehman Brothers, "Proxy Statement for Year-end 2007," p. 28; JP Morgan Chase, "2007 Proxy Statement," p. 16.

[37] FCIC Report (2011), Original Footnote 68: New York State Office of the State Comptroller, "New York City Securities Industry Bonus

Total compensation for the major U.S. banks and securities firms was estimated at $137 billion.[38] (FCIC Report, Page no 91)[39]

In effect, in all these firms, the focus was on the short-term performance, incentives, and compensation, when, in reality, the risks (which existed) were mostly, medium and/or long-term. Of course, the regulator and law and policy-makers sat and watched as compensation soared way beyond acceptable levels and firms started paying as high as 50 percent of their revenues in compensation.

Did not the regulators and policy- and law-makers find it strange that:
a) Goldman Sachs spent between 44 per cent and 49 per cent of its revenue per year on compensation (during the years 2005 to 2008);
b) Morgan Stanley allotted between 46 percent and 59 percent; and
c) Merrill paid out similar percentages in 2005 and 2006, and more importantly, gave as high as 141 percent in 2007 (a year in which it suffered dramatic losses).

What on earth were the regulators and policy and law-makers doing? This is where, again, it is very important for a presidential candidate to forego any close relationships with Wall Street. As the 2008 financial crisis has clearly demonstrated, there is no free lunch.

Pool," February 23, 2010. The bonus pool is for securities industry (NAICS 523) employees who work in New York City.

[38] FCIC Report (2011), Original Footnote 69: "Banks Set for Record Pay, Top Firms on Pace to Award $145 Billion for 2009, Up 18%, WSJ Study Finds," WSJ.com, January 14, 2010.

[39] Financial Crisis Inquiry Report, Final Report Of The National Commission On The Causes Of The Financial And Economic Crisis In The United States, The Financial Crisis Inquiry Commission, 2011, http://fcic-static.law.stanford.edu/cdn_media/fcic-reports/fcic_final_report_full.pdf

Eighth Cause

As the FCIC report correctly argues, a lot of this happened because conflicts of interest were at play and they were, in a big measure, responsible for the financial crisis of 2008. While there are innumerable examples from the FCIC report that I could cite as evidence of conflicts of interest that were responsible for the financial crisis of 2008, one very relevant example from the SEC[40] is given below:

> Another high profile example of conflict of interest in the recent years is the settlement that the SEC reached with Goldman Sachs, in which that firm paid $550 million to settle charges filed by the Commission, and acknowledged that disclosures made in marketing a subprime mortgage product contained incomplete information as they did not disclose the role of a hedge fund client who was taking the opposite side of the trade in the selection of the CDO.[41]

And I quote:

> Goldman acknowledges that the marketing materials for the ABACUS 2007-ACI transaction contained incomplete information. In particular, it was a mistake for the Goldman marketing materials to state that the reference portfolio was "selected by" ACA Management LLC without disclosing the role of Paulson & Co. Inc. in the portfolio selection process and that Paulson's economic interests were adverse to CDO investors. Goldman regrets that the marketing materials did not contain that disclosure.
> (http://www.sec.gov/litigation/litreleases/2010/consent-pr2010-123.pdf , Page 2, point 3)

---

[40] Carlo V. di Florio, 'Conflicts of Interest and Risk Governance', *U.S. Securities and Exchange Commission*, October 22, 2012, https://www.sec.gov/News/Speech/Detail/Speech/1365171491600
[41] Ibid.

Before I close this appendix, I would like to quote the FCIC report[42] one last time:

> Goldman Sachs "Multiplied the Effects of the Collapse in Subprime"
>
> Henry Paulson, the CEO of Goldman Sachs from 1999 until he became secretary of the Treasury in 2006 testified to the FCIC that by the time he became secretary many bad loans already had been issued—"most of the toothpaste was out of the tube"—and that "there really wasn't the proper regulatory apparatus to deal with it."[43] Paulson provided examples: "Subprime mortgages went from accounting for 5 percent of total mortgages in 1994 to 20 percent by 2006. ... Securitization separated originators from the risk of the products they originated." The result, Paulson observed, "was a housing bubble that eventually burst in far more spectacular fashion than most previous bubbles."[44]
>
> Under Paulson's leadership, Goldman Sachs had played a central role in the creation and sale of mortgage securities. From 2004 through 2006, the company provided billions of dollars in loans to mortgage lenders; most went to the subprime lenders Ameriquest, Long Beach, Fremont, New Century, and Countrywide through warehouse lines of credit, often in the form of repos.[45] During the same period, Goldman acquired $ 53 billion of loans from these and other subprime loan

---

[42] Financial Crisis Inquiry Report, Final Report Of The National Commission On The Causes Of The Financial And Economic Crisis In The United States, The Financial Crisis Inquiry Commission, 2011, http://fcic-static.law.stanford.edu/cdn_media/fcic-reports/fcic_final_report_full.pdf

[43] FCIC Report (2011), Original Footnote 96: Henry M. Paulson Jr., testimony before the FCIC, Hearing on the Shadow Banking System, day 2, session 1: Perspective on the Shadow Banking System, May 6, 2010, transcript, p. 22.

[44] FCIC Report (2011), Original Footnote 97: Henry M. Paulson Jr., written testimony for the FCIC, Hearing on the Shadow Banking System, day 2, session 1: Perspective on the Shadow Banking System, May 6, 2010, p. 2.

[45] FCIC Report (2011), Original Footnote 98: Goldman Sachs, 2005 and 2006 10-K (appendix 5a to Goldman's March 8, 2010, letter to the FCIC).

originators, which it securitized and sold to investors.[46] From 2004 to 2006 Goldman issued 318 mortgage securitizations totaling $184 billion (about a quarter were subprime), and 63 CDOs totaling $32 billion; Goldman also issued 22 synthetic or hybrid CDOs with a face value of $35 billion between 2004 and June 2006.[47] (FCIC Report, Page no 170)

To summarize, the FCIC report cites the following as among the key causes of the financial crisis of 2008:

a) The lack of proper regulation and supervision;
b) The lax and laissez-faire attitude of the regulators and law- and policy-makers (due to conflicts of interests);
c) The reckless ride that many Wall Street firms (including investment banks, commercial banks, financial conglomerates etc.) took off on down a highway with no speed limits;
d) The poor operational practices, weak financial condition, and huge compensation packages at many of these Wall Street firms (including investment banks, commercial banks, financial conglomerates etc.);
e) The conflicts of interest that were prevalent in the larger policy, business, and political environment and so on.

---

[46] FCIC Report (2011), Original Footnote 99: Appendix 5c to Goldman's March 8, 2010, letter to the FCIC.
[47] FCIC Report (2011), Original Footnote 100: Goldman's March 8, 2010, letter to the FCIC, p. 28 (subprime securities).

Appendix 7

The 2010 Andhra Pradesh (AP) Microfinance Crisis: Lessons for Various Stakeholders

Unfortunately, in India, financial inclusion has translated merely to the delivery of consumption credit (and some small production loans). That consumption credit alone is insufficient to reduce or alleviate poverty is perhaps a no-brainer, for all honest development practitioners. Despite the lack of serious impact studies, for those who have worked at the grassroots and continue to so, it is evident that mere access to finance cannot and will not help people come out of poverty. Access to finance is, therefore, best viewed as a necessary, but not sufficient, condition for poverty alleviation.

While microfinance professionals and access to finance enthusiasts can perhaps take comfort in the fact that consumption loans alone cannot make a dent on poverty, there is a caveat in order. They cannot escape the fact that the drive and desire to include low-income people with regard to financial services has resulted in the proliferation of financial services focused on loans and even within loans, primarily consumption lending. The enthusiasm to include low-income people has also led to not-so-good practices including multiple lending, over-lending, top-up loans, ghost/*benami* loans, and the like; driven by the motivation of some MFIs to generate huge wealth for themselves and their promoters.

In fact, one of the major reasons for the 2010 AP microfinance crisis was the mindless drive to include people financially, without asking the question(s) on whether the current bouquet of financial services being offered were indeed appropriate, whether the practices being followed were fair, transparent, legal and ethically sound, and whether the other conditions so necessary for effective use of the financial services existed at the grassroots.

Specifically, while MFIs grew for different reasons, it was during this period of burgeoning growth (April 2008–March 2010 and thereafter until September 2010) that the hitherto highly successful model of

JLGs/centres was severely diluted. And the changes did more harm than good to the original concept of joint liability and peer pressure—as several JLGs operated in a mutually reinforcing (cartel-like) manner within a centre.

Four issues are relevant here:

1. One: The normal and established processes of client acquisition through green field methods—where MFIs laboriously promoted their own groups, nurtured them and painstakingly created a culture of credit discipline and high repayment based on mutual trust and other aspects—were slowly abandoned by many MFIs because of their urgency to grow fast. Process mapping, which is a good tool by itself, and efficiency goals, which are laudable, were erroneously used to quicken client acquisition strategies and other related processes. Thus, an undue emphasis was placed on quicker identification of clients, faster processing of loan applications, and so on. And basic issues such as the understanding of a client's antecedents and contextual situations, preparation of clients, analysis of client/household loan absorption and debt-servicing capacity and the like—which were the hallmarks of the green field client-acquisition strategy in the traditional Grameen model—were slowly but surely ignored and bypassed.
2. Two: Given that clients needed to be identified faster and loans disbursed to them quickly, the MFIs concerned had just two options for client acquisition: (i) acquisition—whereby MFIs started taking over the portfolio of smaller MFIs or specific JLGs. Sometimes, SHGs were also taken over (cannibalized) and split into several JLGs (depending on the size of SHG); and (ii) mutual sharing—whereby several MFIs decided to share and use their available JLGs/clients on successive days and on the basis of a simple reciprocal arrangement. While both strategies were used, over time, cartels of MFIs started to follow the latter as it was a win-win situation for all of them.
3. Three: Both of these led to the emergence of power brokers (also called broker agents[48] or ring leaders)—they were basically

---

[48] (a) Implementation safeguards against notorious agents are an imperative for the proposed microfinance bill (http://www.moneylife.in/article/implementation-safeguards-against-notorious-agents-are-an-imperative-for-the-proposed-microfinance-bill/19017.html) by Ramesh S. Arunachalam, August 18, 2011; (b) How and why did microfinance agents become a part

centre leaders (or sometimes, even group leaders, loan officers, and local political honchos) who had access to a captive set of JLGs and clients. These new intermediaries started to matchmake with different MFIs on increasingly attractive and exploitative terms. Thus, slowly, these agents became the most powerful pivot in the local microfinance system and various processes were outsourced to them, often without any quality checks. The outsourced processes ranged from client acquisition to KYC documentation, loan disbursement, repayment collection, and so on. Over time, this outsourcing through agents became an established strategy and the agents became omnipresent and omnipotent in the Indian microfinance industry. They often demanded their pound of flesh and got it, too. It appears that the coercive practices and multiple lending, which have often been cited in the 2010 AP crisis, were due to the presence and use of such agents. It is also clear that, given the burgeoning growth and prevalence of such agent-led decentralized microfinance models, it would be difficult to enforce concepts like social performance[49] on the ground.

4. Four: Over the period April 2008–March 2010 and thereafter, growth did not come from adding fresh clients. Rather, it came through concurrent loans (from the same MFI) to its clients and multiple lending[50] to shared JLGs/clients, who were serviced by different MFIs on different days. In fact, data reveal that for the six large AP-headquartered NBFC MFIs, while their clients grew by about 1.30 times across two reference periods (April 2008–March 2009 and April 2009–March 2010), the growth in gross

---

of the Indian microfinance business?
(http://www.moneylife.in/article/how-and-why-did-microfinance-agents-become-a-part-of-the-indian-microfinance-business/19301.html) by Ramesh S. Arunachalam, August 29, 2011; and (c) Implementation safeguards against notorious agents are an imperative for the proposed microfinance bill
(http://www.moneylife.in/article/implementation-safeguards-against-notorious-agents-are-an-imperative-for-the-proposed-microfinance-bill/19017.html) by Ramesh S. Arunachalam, August 18, 2011.

[49] Microfinance: Will seal of excellence and social performance management as yardsticks work?, Ramesh S Arunachalam, September 24, 2011, http://www.moneylife.in/article/microfinance-will-seal-of-excellence-and-social-performance-management-as-yardsticks-work/20038.html

[50] Also ghost lending.

loan portfolio across these two periods was about 2.19^{51} times, indicating that portfolio deepening had occurred perhaps through larger or successive or multiple loans to the clients.

These concurrent and parallel MFI loans, through shared JLGs and clients, appeared to be a godsend and clients just grabbed them during the phase of burgeoning growth—as by then many of them realized that they could not service their increasing debt. The cases of Zaheera Bhee^{52} and others clearly illustrate this. The MFIs too were ecstatic about turbo charging financial inclusion and so were equity investors, banks, regulators/supervisors, policymakers, and other stakeholders including international bodies such as the CGAP. This is a critical point that needs to be noted. The outreach of the Indian microfinance industry even today needs significant correction and revision to reflect this reality of concurrent loans, ghost loans and multiple loans to shared JLGs/clients.

Therefore, it is high time that we recognize and use the following lessons (from the Indian microfinance crisis) with regard to promoting inclusive finance for low-income people, in India and globally:

---

^{51} This should have been higher at 2.47 had the Mix Market retained the original GLP figures that it had put out in 2010/2011 for BASIX and SHARE. For some reason, Mix Market changed its original figures for BASIX and SHARE respectively from US$ 223,229,799 and US$ for 490,923,201 to US$ 172,484,946 and US$ 376,593,362. I have the original print screen data and other pieces of evidence with regard to the original data put out by Mix Market. There are several other issues with the Mix Market database and I can provide the details if required.
^{52} http://microfinance-in-india.blogspot.com/2010/11/can-we-bring-back-ayeshas-ammy.html

Lesson # 1: The scope of current inclusive finance practice in India is rather narrow. While the intentions (like the report of the Financial Inclusion Committee and other policy pronouncements) may have been to provide low-income clients with access to a wide range of need-based financial services, in reality, the inclusive finance (or financial inclusion) paradigm[53] has mainly led to the proliferation of credit and primarily, consumption loans, although there have been some small production/livelihood loans.

Lesson # 2: Standard (MFI) loans for consumption and/or small production needs, which dominate microfinance (or access to finance) in India today, tend to work well for loan sizes in the range of Rs. 10,000–Rs. 15,000 per client and at most <= Rs. 50,000.

Lesson # 3: Rs. 50,000 as the loan amount is some sort of *Lakshman Reka*,[54] that the MFIs should not breach, unless they are absolutely sure of the individual/household having the requisite debt servicing ability (could be a livelihood, production unit, and/or labour, etc.) to repay the larger loan. This is the most important lesson from the 2010 AP crisis for MFIs, banks, policymakers, regulators/supervisors, and other stakeholders.

Lesson # 4: Indiscriminate (and multiple) lending to low-income people under the pretext of furthering financial inclusion—without regard to their (and their families) loan absorption and debt servicing capacity, and especially in the wake of vulnerable livelihoods, can only prove to be a recipe for disaster. As has been demonstrated by the 2010 AP crisis, this will ultimately exclude them altogether from the financial system. As has been argued, when people with weak and

---

[53] In India, typically, financial inclusion (FI) is presently characterized by (i) preoccupation with opening of savings accounts; (ii) large focus on consumption credit and small production loans; (iii) low outreach with regard to vulnerable groups in agriculture; (iv) lack of suitable and affordable risk management services; and (v) lack of appropriate livelihood financing. The two aspects of lack of suitable and affordable risk management services and lack of appropriate and affordable livelihood financing are noteworthy aspects because they again show the huge gaps between a great vision and intended strategy (the recommendation of the well-intentioned Financial Inclusion Committee) and actual implementation on the ground, which is narrowly focused on consumption and small production credit.

[54] A popular metaphor for a line not to be crossed.

vulnerable livelihoods are loaned large sums of money (> Rs. 50,000), repayment will either have to come from fresh loans (i.e., greening through concurrent/multiple lending) and/or restructuring of loans. At some point, this cycle will (have to) stop and the bubble will simply burst. These clients will then become financially excluded all over again.

If that is the scenario, what can nodal institutions do to help the microfinance industry overcome this precarious situation? First, they can help re-engineer the financial inclusion paradigm, to address some of the issues mentioned here. In my opinion, this reengineering should ensure the delivery of quality credit that will reduce risk and vulnerability of low-income clients and give them more choices.[55]

By quality credit, I am arguing for a greater focus on post-harvest and/or post-production financing for agriculture and other sectors that provide (or can provide) significant livelihoods opportunities for low-income people. In other words, among other things, this would call for the financing of agriculture produce/other products[56] marketing—a very critical aspect for small/marginal producers[57] as it has the potential to enhance choices for them in terms of buyers, and so on.

Of course, here, the existing relationships would need to be better understood if financial products are to be developed and delivered through appropriate channels.[58] Second, these nodal agencies must ensure that the focus of financial inclusion is reengineered such that the delivery of a wide range of financial services (loans, savings, insurance, pensions, etc.) are used strategically to drive higher rewards, better remuneration, and greater power down the value chain—otherwise, it will be of limited use.

---

[55] This can happen through alternative channels that afford lower costs, have greater trust, and high levels of mutual acceptance.
[56] Like handicrafts, etc.
[57] MSMEs as well.
[58] And this would need to be validated specifically for a context, a product, and a partner but these are general suggested arrangements.

Hence, they need to help initiate a new microfinance paradigm[59] where financial products, mechanisms, and instruments can be used to perform the following:

- Reduce risk/vulnerability[60] in the existing livelihoods of low-income people, arising from various market imperfections—examples include warehouse receipt financing implemented with appropriate safeguards, pro-poor value-chain financing, and so on;

- Help create strong safety and security nets[61] for these low-income clients for a range of aspects including various insurance and risk mitigation products;

- Enable these low-income clients to pursue diversified/migratory livelihoods where required;

- Facilitate re-inclusion of these low-income people (who were once included but subsequently excluded because of fragile livelihoods); and

- Create risk management mechanisms[62] to ensure that they continue to stay financially included, in the context of their fragile livelihoods.

---

[59] Source: Adapted from Arunachalam, Ramesh S, "UNDP Financial Inclusion Strategy in 7 Focus States: Strategic Consideration and Suggestions, UNDP," 2007.
[60] Weather and crop insurance are gaining ground. Contract farming schemes exist but are not producer oriented.
[61] Some innovations exist here for health as well as life coverage but much work is necessary in the nature of product design and also distribution. Micro-pension schemes are also available.
[62] Post harvest loans in fisheries/agriculture and warehouse receipts are examples of such products.

Thus, I would very much like the nodal agencies to champion the larger cause of reengineering the financial inclusion paradigm to facilitate poverty alleviation on the ground. I am sure they have the wherewithal and resources to do this. Let us hope their governance structure and senior management take this appeal seriously and demonstrate sufficient will to do this in real time, on the ground.

Interestingly, much of what happened in Andhra Pradesh in 2010 is now replicating itself in other states of India. Whether a pan India microfinance crisis will unfold or not, is an aspect that time alone can answer!

About the Author

Ramesh S Arunachalam wears many hats. He is an Industrial Engineer from the National Institute of Technology (NIT), Trichy, India and an MBA (with Dual Concentration, Strategy and Marketing) from the Carlson School of Management, University of Minnesota, Minneapolis, USA. In the last 30 years, he has been a columnist with the Hindu Business Line (1995-97) and Moneylife (2011-2013), a development practitioner and strategic advisor. He has worked in a wide range of areas including financial sector regulation and supervision, financial inclusion, microfinance, livelihoods and MSMEs, Gender and microfinance, ERP systems for microfinance and infrastructure finance, urban development, infrastructure financing, GIS for urban planning and e Governance.

During the last 30 years, Ramesh has completed 308 professional assignments. He has worked in 614 districts of India and has also travelled and worked extensively in about 26 countries in North America, Asia, Africa, Europe and the Caribbean across diverse projects (in senior positions). He is passionate about his work and brings strong inter-disciplinary insight to his assignments. His clients include governments (Governments of India, St Lucia, Singapore, Malawi, Uganda, Philippines, Afghanistan etc, several State Governments in India and many GoI Institutions like NCRPB, SIDBI, NABARD etc), bi-lateral agencies (DFID, USAID, DANIDA, NORAD, SIDA etc), multi-lateral agencies (UNDP, World Bank, ADB, IFAD, The Commonwealth Secretariat etc), regulators, commercial banks, investment banks, microfinance institutions, private sector firms and several other stakeholders globally.

He has authored numerous reports/studies/papers as part of his assignments, several of which have been published internationally and received global recognition. His blog on microfinance has been well received and he has also penned two books in microfinance and financial inclusion—**The Journey of Indian Microfinance: Lessons for the Future** and **An Idea Which Went Wrong: Commercial Microfinance in India**—both of which have received critical acclaim. His first novel is an entertaining crime thriller—**Where Angels Prey**—released in April 2015 through AuthorsUpFront, which again was well received. His non-fiction writing continued with critically acclaimed popular books over the last five years—**"Madam President: History in the Making?"**, **"Dirty Money: The U.S. Presidential Elections 2016"**, **"The Cinderella Notes: Demonetization and The Indian Economy"**, **"9/11: The Unanswered Questions"**, **"Powering A Billion Dreams: Towards A New Financial Inclusion Paradigm**, **"Never Waste A Crisis: Towards A Stable Financial Sector"**, **"Piercing The Corporate Veil: Towards An Accountable Financial Sector"** and **"Central Banks: Mandates, Autonomy and Accountability"** (see www.amazon.com).

Title – **Where Angels Prey**
Author – Ramesh S Arunachalam
Size – 5.5 inches × 8.5 inches
No of Pages – 204
Binding – Paperback
ISBN – 978-9384439378

While the rest of the world reels under a severe financial crisis, India's microfinance sector enjoys an unprecedented boom. Why on earth are people investing such huge amounts of money in an obscure industry, especially at the time of global recession? And why is Wall Street suddenly so interested in India's poor?

That is exactly what Robert Bradlee, senior correspondent with *The New York Post*, sets off to investigate, along with his journalist friend, Chandresh. Little does he know that his search for a scoop would lead him through a complex multi-pronged web of deceit, fraud, manipulation and financial crime, remote controlled from distant lands by an entire chain of financial sector stakeholders.

Gripping, racy and meticulously researched, this financial thriller weaves in and out of the affluent world of high-powered boardrooms and the gruelling poverty of the remotest villages of India, to reveal the devastating truths that often lurk behind "good intentions".

www.ingramcontent.com/pod-product-compliance
Lightning Source LLC
Chambersburg PA
CBHW030613220526
45463CB00004B/1275